The First 100 Days of Platoon Leadership

Handbook

Lessons and Best Practices

The First 100 Days of Platoon Leadership

DIGITAL VERSION AVAILABLE

A digital version of this CALL publication is available to view or download from the CALL website:

http://call.army.mil

Reproduction of this publication is welcomed and highly encouraged.

FOLLOW CALL ON SOCIAL MEDIA

https://twitter.com/USArmy_CALL
https://www.facebook.com/CenterforArmyLessonsLearned

Foreword

The platoon leader and platoon sergeant are two of the most important leaders in the U.S. Army. The way platoon leaders and sergeants work together as a team can cause the success or failure of companies, battalions, brigades, and divisions. They represent the leading edge of leadership on and off the battlefield.

On the battlefield, platoon leaders and sergeants build their platoons, empower squad leaders, integrate outside elements, and use troop-leading procedures to plan and lead. Off the battlefield, platoon leaders and sergeants prepare their platoon for combat through tough training. The platoon leader and platoon sergeant's ability to coach, teach, and mentor their Soldiers leads directly to the readiness of our formations.

World-wide, platoon leaders and sergeants are personally leading the U.S. Army at the lowest level. This handbook is a guide for new leaders to help prepare them for a critical crucible of leadership that will determine the U.S. Army's ability to fight and win our country's wars.

MICHAEL F. PAPPAL
COL, AR
Director, Center for Army Lessons Learned

The First 100 Days of Platoon Leadership

Table of Contents

Center For Army Lessons Learned

Director	COL Michael F. Pappal
CALL Analyst	CPT David B. Beale
Contributors	CPT Drew Paulson
	CPT Heath Kennedy
	CPT Peter Chun

Special thanks to the active members of the Junior Officer Forum for their contributions and dedication to the profession at arms, available online at https://juniorofficer.army.mil/.

The Secretary of the Army has determined that the publication of this periodical is necessary in the transaction of the public business as required by law of the Department.

Unless otherwise stated, whenever the masculine or feminine gender is used, both are intended.

Note: Any publications (other than CALL publications) referenced in this product, such as ARs, ADPs, ADRPs, ATPs, FMs, and TMs, must be obtained through your pinpoint distribution system.

Introduction

> *"There are a few relationships you will remember for the rest of your life: your first sergeant, your command sergeant major, and most importantly, your platoon sergeant."*
>
> — Former division commander

Purpose

Noncommissioned Officer Professional Development System (NCOPDS)/ Officer Education System (OES) schools have neither the time nor ability to cover every scenario a new platoon leader (PL) or platoon sergeant (PSG) may face after assuming duties. The Center for Army Lessons Learned, in conjunction with serving and former PLs and PSGs, has compiled lessons learned and best practices for PLs and PSGs and those who aspire to these positions to improve themselves and their units. The purpose of this handbook is to provide these lessons learned and best practices to PLs and PSGs to help enable their success in their first 100 days in position and beyond.

For Platoon Leaders

To earn your commission, you have undergone extensive training and are better trained and more prepared to be a PL than you know. In addition to basic combat skills, you have been trained and tested to lead leaders, manage organizations, and integrate combined arms to defeat the enemy. This handbook will educate you on how to build on your training and work with NCOs. Never forget you are responsible for Soldiers' lives, the most precious resource in the Army, and must make tough decisions. Also, never forget you have an NCO support chain.

For Platoon Sergeants

You have been a Soldier, team leader, squad leader, and earned a wealth of experience. This knowledge will inform and prepare you to be a PSG. This handbook will educate you on how to build on current experience and work with a partner PL, something team and squad leaders do not have to do. Never forget you are responsible for Soldiers' lives, the most precious resource in the Army, and must prepare them for the mission. Also, never forget you are part of a leadership team; you and your PL sink or swim together.

About This Handbook

This handbook consists of five chapters and two appendices:

Chapter 1, Leadership, discusses leadership at the platoon level for PLs and PSGs. It includes information on how to empower squad leaders, counsel subordinates, and how PLs and PSGs manage their noncommissioned officer (NCO)/officer relationship and duties.

Chapter 2, Platoon Training, discusses platoon training such as how to train and prepare Soldiers for collective training and the planning and resourcing of platoon training events.

Chapter 3, Knowledge, outlines knowledge a PL and PSG need to prepare their unit for success. It discusses how to maintain platoon equipment, manage property, build cohesion, deal with discipline, and contribute to a company's family readiness program.

Chapter 4, Execution, discusses the platoon's actions during execution. It includes how to plan using troop-leading procedures, lead a patrol, integrate enablers, and leverage after action reviews to improve the platoon.

Chapter 5, Vignettes, consists of platoon vignettes that discuss situations encountered by leaders. They are designed for use as part of leader development discussions. Young leaders may deal with these situations during their first 100 days.

Note: Throughout this handbook is a series of color-coded boxes containing lessons learned and best practices.

For Platoon Leaders

The blue boxes contain lessons learned and best practices specifically for PLs.

For Platoon Sergeants

The yellow boxes contain lessons learned and best practices specifically for PSGs.

For Platoon Leaders and Platoon Sergeants

The green boxes contain lessons learned and best practices for both PLs and PSGs.

Chapter 1
Leadership

Overview

A platoon leader (PL) and platoon sergeant's (PSG's) primary job is to inspire and influence their platoon to accomplish the mission. They do this by providing purpose, direction, and motivation to accomplish the mission and improve the organization.[1] PLs and PSGs are responsible for all missions their platoon accomplishes or fails. This responsibility comes with the position, but they are only successful because of character, presence, and intellect.

This chapter discusses assumption of the first platoon-level leadership role, building a team, effective versus ineffective leadership, PL and PSG duties, using squad leaders, effective counseling at the platoon level, engaged leadership, time and task management for a platoon, and insights on mission command.

Assumption of the First Platoon-Level Leadership Role

"*During my first 100 days, a variation of competencies in junior leaders and difficulty in understanding my commander's priorities and guidance surprised me. People really need to be prepared to take control of an organization on day one and soak everything in.*"

— Former infantry PL

A Soldier's first impression of a leader has a lasting impact throughout his time as a leader. This is especially true at the platoon level. Whether there is an effective relief-in-place process or none, Soldiers remember if a leader takes charge and is organized. When assuming a platoon, leaders need to take charge; assess their manning, equipment, and training status; determine expectations of themselves; learn the strengths and weaknesses of subordinates; and communicate their expectations for their unit.

PLs and PSGs run platoons. This may be the first time the PL or PSG is in a leadership position at the platoon level, which may cause feelings of inexperience or doubt. Army leaders can rely on the Army values — Loyalty, Duty, Respect, Selfless Service, Honor, Integrity, and Personal Courage — as a guide to take charge. New leaders should immediately be responsible to their higher headquarters and listen to subordinate leaders. New PLs and PSGs should also trust their instinct; as leaders, they are duty bound to look deeper into an issue they do not feel is correct. When a leader identifies something that needs to change during their first 100 days — unless it is unsafe, illegal, or immoral and needs to be immediately addressed — they should work with their platoon to develop an action plan for improvement over time.

> "*Our No. 1 task, bar none, remains readiness. Readiness for what? Readiness for war. Readiness for the intense combat of ground operations of any type, anywhere in the world. That is our task. And I can tell you that it has never been more important than it is today.*"
>
> — GEN Mark A. Milley, Chief of Staff of the U.S. Army, 10 October 2017[2]

It is a PL and PSG's duty to maintain the readiness of their platoons. When assuming command of their platoon, leaders must understand where their platoon stands from their partner (PL/PSG) and make their own assessment. PSGs typically determine manning at the platoon level, but a Soldier-by-Soldier review should be done between a PL and PSG to review strengths or gaps. Leaders can use their initial accountability inventory of their equipment to assess discipline, equipment maintenance, and readiness of a platoon. Leaders should involve themselves immediately in supervising sergeant's time and individual training to assess their element's readiness. New leaders should not assume their platoon is at the walk stage just because they are new. Leaders need to accurately assess where their platoon is and plan appropriate training.

For Platoon Leaders

As a PL, your expectations come from both your company and battalion commanders. They may come in the form of formal counseling or informal direction. You receive guidance from higher leaders and translate this guidance to your platoon. Spend the time on clarifying expectations, provide backbriefs, and understand how your platoon fits into the company and battalion's bigger picture as you assume command of your platoon.

For Platoon Sergeants

As a PSG, your expectations come from your PL, commander, first sergeant (1SG), and command sergeant major (CSM). Normally, these sources are synchronized, but if not, you must coordinate with your PL to determine what is expected of your platoon. This is a spot where PLs and PSGs get into trouble. You both may have a different understanding of higher leadership's expectations. Communication is the key. As the senior noncommissioned officer (NCO) and mentor, take time with your PL and, as a team, determine and record what is expected of your platoon for standards, training, and mission execution. This common understanding of expectations will build your individual relationship and your platoon's ability to focus on what is most important.

PLs and PSGs rely on their squad leaders. Spending the time to review each subordinate leader's strengths and weaknesses is key. Who is better at administrative functions and who is better in the field? Which leader can be given less guidance to execute a task and who needs to be given additional direction and supervision? This assessment will help build a team and ensure the right people are given the right tasks to accomplish.

Finally, leaders need to lay out expectations for their platoon and what their platoon can expect of their leaders. This should happen formally through the counseling process and informally by example. PLs and PSGs must "walk the walk and talk the talk," showing both integrity and technical knowledge to their Soldiers. Ideally, this should come from both the PL and PSG, showing unity of command.

A leader's first 100 days can make or break their leadership experience. Many leaders who make a poor impression are never able to overcome their Soldiers' loss of confidence in them. Build up leadership equity at the start by communicating and enforcing standards early and often. In addition to the technical and tactical knowledge expected of Army leaders, they are expected to model and enforce the Army values. PLs and PSGs must take charge, communicate, and continuously assess their platoon's readiness, expectations from higher, the strengths and weaknesses of their platoon, and set baseline expectations and standards for their platoon.

Building the Team

> "*In my experience, shared hardship is the most effective way to obtain team cohesion … . Once a group conquers a shared hardship through teamwork, its members develop mutual trust and confidence in one another.*"
>
> — Former Security Forces Assistance team lieutenant[3]

A functional platoon requires a cohesive team. Exercising mission command and empowering junior leaders requires teams that are built through mutual trust. Platoon-level leaders gain this mutual trust through building a team based on shared experiences, enforcing standards, creating a platoon identity, building trust in training environments, and having a welcome program. A platoon where leaders do not share hardships may not function as well.

> **For Platoon Leaders and Platoon Sergeants**
>
> Building your platoon team starts with your relationship. In a platoon where the PL and PSG have interpersonal issues or a lack of trust, the platoon's cohesion and ability to operate will degrade. Soldiers often choose sides, hindering your ability to lead. Consider discussing this during your initial counseling. Soldiers who can detect a rift between the platoon team will be quick to exploit it and undermine the PL and PSG.

One proven method of building a platoon team is through shared experiences. Tough physical training and field exercises require a platoon to work together to be successful. As Soldiers feel they hit their individual limits, they often look for motivation from those around them. As they see members of their platoon persevere, Soldiers gain confidence in their team and can usually push themselves further. Executing combat-focused physical training with ruck marches, litter and buddy carries, and other events bring Soldiers in a platoon closer together. Similarly in the field, Soldiers in the platoon who plan and execute tough collective training gain confidence in each other's abilities and form a closer team.

A great resource for platoons is the local Morale, Welfare, and Recreation (MWR) program. High-ropes courses, paintball, or other MWR excursions are beneficial opportunities that create shared hardships and team building. Most companies have access to MWR funds to supplement the cost of morale and team-building events.

Another method of team building is consistent, high standards. Soldiers in a cohesive team have ownership of and buy into their platoon. Creating and enforcing high physical, tactical, and discipline standards motivates Soldiers and can make them feel like an elite unit able to achieve more than their sister platoons. Some platoons develop a qualification program, mixing physical and tactical tasks. These programs are effective at establishing high standards and esprit de corps. However, programs must be achievable and must not exclude Soldiers, which may lead to hazing. Externally, inter-platoon competition has its benefits, but taken to extremes, it can become unhealthy. Unhealthy competition results in the loss of cohesion (for example, when winning by any means leads to unethical decisions or when it separates a platoon as a non-team player with the company, adversely affecting company cohesion).

As the platoon starts to work together and gain confidence as a team, a platoon's identity and culture will grow. This culture is a direct reflection of the PL and PSG. Platoon leadership that models the Army values; works hard; maintains open communication; and does not accept bullying, harassment, and hazing builds a positive culture. Often, unit identity is built around a common symbol or motto. New leaders often try to put their own influence on the platoon to reflect their vision. Leaders should be wary of making immediate identity changes as they assume their position. It sounds simple to change a symbol, call sign, or motto, but these are symbols that team cohesion is built around. By changing them, new leaders may show a lack of interest in the platoon's identity. Of course, if there is already a cohesion problem or these symbols have a negative impact, new PLs and PSGs must swiftly and decisively change them to start the culture shift.

Cohesive teams prepare for execution by building trust in training environments. PLs and PSGs should empower squad and team leaders to lead during training. Challenging junior leaders in training enables platoon-level leaders to mentor and train them to execute tasks independently when needed. Leaders take advantage of Sergeant's Time Training (STT), opportunity training, and field exercises to provide Soldiers the opportunity to learn but to also demonstrate their skills, gaining the trust of their peers.

Most companies have a sponsorship and welcome program run by the 1SG. Platoon-level leaders should support the company program and expand on it at the platoon level. The PL or PSG should sit down with each incoming Soldier, provide them standards and expectations, and get to know them. Learning an incoming Soldier's hobbies, professional and personal background, family members, and habits builds rapport between Soldiers and their leaders. This rapport allows leaders to know their Soldiers and welcome them to the platoon. It will also enable a leader to spot when there is something wrong with a Soldier. It is often difficult to do this due to competing priorities, but if either the PL or PSG cannot do this immediately, they should follow up as soon as possible.

For Platoon Sergeants

The platoon welcome program is usually run by the PSG. You are often the first leader a Soldier meets and interacts with. How you welcome and incorporate new Soldiers into your platoon will have a lasting impact on the culture of your platoon and company. Take time to talk with your PL about the culture the platoon wants to project to new Soldiers and how you will achieve that. Record your plan either as a memorandum for record or on a counseling form. Being proactive will identify and prevent issues down the road.

A platoon is a team built on experience and trust. Platoon-level leaders who recognize this build trust through shared experiences, high standards, creating a platoon identity, empowering Soldiers in training environments, and having an effective welcome program. Building and maintaining a team allows platoons to accomplish their mission during training and execution.

Effective Versus Ineffective Leadership

> *"Sir, you know how to plan; it doesn't matter what your orders are. We are here to execute. Most importantly though, you have to give [those orders] confidently."*
>
> — PSG to a new PL

Platoon leadership needs to work as a team to be effective. There are multiple types and styles of leadership, but there are key elements of effective and ineffective leadership. The following are examples of both effective and ineffective leadership experienced by previous PLs and PSGs.

Effective Leadership

> **Take Charge**
>
> After arriving at my first duty station, I was driven out to the field by my executive officer (XO) and dropped off with the battalion's support platoon. I had never met the PSG or any of the Soldiers before. Within the first day, one of my Soldiers lost his night vision goggles (NVGs) because they weren't tied down. My PSG was a young staff sergeant (SSG) and I had to step up. First, I inspected the platoon's tie downs and then worked out a plan turning the platoon out searching for the equipment. Second, I went and reported to the commander that we had lost a pair of NVGs. Eventually, we located the equipment and I ended up having the Soldier re-tie the entire platoon's NVG tie downs. When we came out of the field, the platoon knew I was in charge and expected nothing but the best from them. My commander knew he could trust me to keep him informed and take responsibility for my platoon's actions. I learned a lot from that first field problem and I've used what I learned from that experience the rest of my career.
>
> — Current company commander

Build the Team

I've always been a gym rat as a Soldier. Once I became a PSG I was a bit overwhelmed, so I changed my schedule to hit the gym before company physical training. Looking back, this was one of the best actions I took. My squad and team leaders started joining me for my pre-physical training sessions. During this time, just as a platoon, my junior leaders could relax and get to know each other in ways you just can't during the duty day. When the brigade went to the Joint Readiness Training Center (JRTC), I knew I could trust each of my team and squad leaders to get the mission done.

— Former PSG

Set the Standard

When I was in Kuwait, my battalion was on recall but we often had a lot of downtime. When we were off, I tended to take my Soldiers to the gym or focus on planning our next training event. There were some PLs who spent a lot of time playing video games in their bunks. Soldiers would see them playing during their downtime and when we were training you could see those PLs struggle leading their platoon. I learned that Soldiers are always watching leaders and you need to always maintain a high personal standard.

— PL after returning from Kuwait

Back Each Other Up

As a new PL, I took charge of my platoon during my deployment in Afghanistan. A couple days in on patrol, I received a change of mission from the battalion, moving us to a hotter area where we had taken contact the week prior. When I gave a warning order (WARNORD) over the radio, one of my team leaders came back questioning the wisdom of my order over the platoon net. At first I wasn't sure what to do. My PSG came on the net and backed me up, telling the team leader to back down and listen for the rest of the WARNORD. After that, I knew my PSG would always back me up and he built confidence in me as a leader.

— Former PL

Knowing About Their Soldiers

When new Soldiers arrived at the platoon, I would always counsel them. I wanted to know as much about my men as possible so we could build a relationship: where they live, what their personal life was like, and what their hobbies were. One afternoon before the National Training Center, one of my Soldiers gave me a call and wanted to talk. His wife was leaving with the kids. It took me about 30 seconds to determine he was thinking about hurting himself from how he was talking and I knew he had a weapon in the house.

My PSG and I linked up and headed to his house to meet him and we spent all night with the Soldier talking about his family. I believe to this day, if I was not as engaged with my Soldier, if we didn't build trust, and if I did not take the time to answer that phone call, I would have spent the next couple weeks planning a memorial service instead of visiting my Soldier in the hospital.

— Current PL

Build a Relationship

My first PSG, a combat veteran, told me that I needed to counsel him. As a second lieutenant (2LT) how could I counsel a veteran with multiple deployments? So I asked him what questions he had for me. He said he had only one: Did I want him to work for me or with me? Being the naive 2LT, I asked him what did it mean to work for me? He said he would follow my orders and accomplish any mission given to him to the best of his ability to make our platoon combat ready. I thought that sounded pretty good, so I asked him what it means to work with me? He said he would follow my orders and accomplish any mission given to him to the best of his ability and do anything else he thought necessary based on his experience to make our platoon combat ready. Of course, I thought that sounded better. Obviously, he was asking for me to empower him and to learn from him without directly stating that. I have kept that lesson (actually multiple lessons) with me to this day.

— Former special forces commander

Ineffective Leadership

Unwilling to Listen

When planning our first small arms range as officer in charge (OIC)/noncommissioned officer in charge (NCOIC), my PL and I went over the plan multiple times. I recommended we work a chow/water plan into the range, making time in the timeline for chow and having a water buffalo on-site. My PL, just out of Ranger school, wanted the platoon to eat on the move and carry water. Despite me telling him the commander would not go for it, he briefed his plan during the training meeting. The commander came down on him. Luckily, I was able to support my PL, telling the commander we would rotate Soldiers off the line for chow and that I had planned to take water cans out with us. After our first range, we started working better together, but it was difficult to overcome his lack of trust in me.

— Military police PSG

Vague Orders

When I took over as PL, my battalion was on red cycle and we had Soldiers supporting multiple taskings from the platoon. It was hard to get all the squad leaders together daily for meetings. I decided to start sending out updates and taskings by text so we could all share information in real time. This worked for a couple days until I sent out "I need two vehicles dispatched Tuesday by 0900 to support a company preparing a defense in training area (TA) 16." My squad leaders dispatched two interim high-mobility engineer excavators (IHMEEs). These are great for digging individual fighting positions but the company wanted vehicle fighting positions. After getting chewed out, I started a 1600 meeting with all squad leaders and team leaders. At times, not everyone was there, but the time spent face-to-face with my NCOs really helped us communicate better.

— Engineer PL

Trust but do not Verify

I remember one of my first high-profile ranges. We were executing a mine-clearing line charge (MICLIC) breach that required special platoon equipment. In the rush to get out to the range I overlooked precombat inspections (PCIs) trusting my squad leaders to handle equipment. Once out on the range, I quickly realized the platoon didn't have what we needed and wasn't prepared for their mission. Luckily, this was training, but I learned that a PL needs to be involved during PCIs for key equipment.

— Combat arms PL

Disagreement Between the PL and PSG

I got a new PL when we were in Afghanistan before I went on mid-tour leave. When I came back, my 1SG was frustrated that my platoon could not go on mission. I asked why and was told that my PL told the commander the platoon was untrained and not prepared for combat missions. We had already been in country for six months and had been executing daily patrols. How my PL assessed us untrained is still a mystery to me. I sat down with the commander and went through our platoon's readiness and status and he lifted the restriction on us. That PL and I started off on a rough foot. I wish he and I would have talked before he gave his assessment to the commander. We ended up having issues working together as a team the rest of deployment.

— Former PSG

Platoon Leader and Platoon Sergeant Duties

> *"PL/PSG relationships are essential, yet complicated. On one hand, you have to immediately lead and establish a professional relationship ... On the other hand, it is your job ... to learn about your Soldiers' lives (especially the senior NCOs), build trust with them, and their respect will come later through the decisions you make on a daily basis and in the field. The goal is to establish a mutual trust that is present in garrison, the field, and in a combat zone."*
>
> — PL during Operation Inherent Resolve (Iraq)

PLs and PSGs are a team. They work together to execute their platoon's mission and success will depend on mutual trust and knowing their partner will do what they need to do. Listed below are ways to delegate tasks, although duties may change based on personalities.

Platoon Leader Duties

- Responsible for what the platoon does or fails to do
- Are the point of contact between the company commander and the platoon; receive mission for the platoon and communicate needs to the commander
- Communicate with higher headquarters for reporting and receipt of mission
- Lead planning
- Develop the concept of the operation
- Lead rehearsals
- Responsible for property
- Develop junior leaders
- Plan training with company leadership

Platoon Sergeant Duties

- Advise PLs
- Are the senior mentors to the platoon
- Track personnel and platoon readiness
- Lead Soldier counseling
- Plan physical training
- Contribute to planning
- Develop maintenance, medical, and supply plans
- Communicate through the XO and 1SG
- Plan packing lists
- Set the standard for equipment and discipline
- Are the lead trainers for the platoon
- Responsible for platoon manning
- Mentor NCOs for career development

Using Your Squad Leaders

"Always listen to your NCOs; however, in the end, you will be the one who makes the overall decision. Be confident in your final choice. If you constantly go back and forth on standards or during decision points, your Soldiers will lose trust in you and your ability to lead."

— Former cavalry PL

Whether operating centralized or distributed as a platoon, platoon leadership relies on squad leaders for mission execution. Squad leaders assist in planning, execute rehearsals, perform precombat checks (PCCs), interact daily with Soldiers, and effectively train individual Soldiers. They are integral to a high-performing platoon. Successful PLs and PSGs influence squad leaders to get the job done.

Squad leaders are critical during planning. Oftentimes, PLs plan in a vacuum and bring in their NCOs either too late in the process or not at all. This type of planning overlooks the collective years of experience that NCOs have. Planning should be a team effort where squad leaders provide input to the PL based on their experience. After given a task and purpose, having squad leaders backbrief their aspect of the operation or actions on the objective can allow valuable bottom-up refinement during planning.

The PL leads and is responsible for planning. PLs should delegate what they can, but need to make the final decision. Platoon-level leaders must be confident in their decisions and not flexible on standards or at a decision point. Indecisiveness and flexible standards undermine platoon leadership and make PLs and PSGs ineffective.

While PLs and PSGs hold and supervise rehearsals for actions on the objective and other key parts of an operation, squad leaders should also be given time to rehearse. Special teams, actions on contact for the lead squad, or even radio procedures are important for squad leaders to review with their squad before a platoon-level rehearsal.

In addition to rehearsals before mission, squad leaders perform PCCs. Having a squad leader backbrief his key squad equipment and status will allow PLs to focus on key platoon equipment during their precombat inspection. Successful platoon leadership empowers squad leaders to hold rehearsals and execute internal PCCs. PLs and PSGs cannot be negligent in their responsibilities and must "trust but verify" their squad leaders, ensuring rehearsals and PCCs are conducted to standard. Building expectations of thoroughness in garrison will help platoon leaders during time-constrained situations in the field or when deployed.

PLs and PSGs should know the amount of time it takes to accomplish specific tasks for their platoon. This allows them to check on their squads without micromanaging. Over-checking subordinates wastes time and focus. This matters in garrison and in the field. Asking for status updates every few minutes directs the squad leader's focus to reporting and not on the mission. In addition, knowing how long it takes to accomplish specific tasks allows platoon-level leaders to keep the company informed without bothering squads.

Both in garrison and in the field, squad leaders are the daily face of the platoon to the Soldiers. Platoon leadership uses morning huddles and afternoon backbriefs to synchronize the platoon. Platoon leadership should empower squad leaders with some training and minor discipline issues but they also need a system to remain informed. "I don't know" or "SGT Hobb's has it" are not acceptable answers when a commander or 1SG talk to a PL or PSG.[4] Leadership is expected to know who, what, where, when, why, and how of its platoon. However, PLs and PSGs cannot be expected to know every detail at all times. Sometimes the answer is "Let me get an update and I will report back."

To stay informed, PLs and PSGs should learn what the company and battalion expect and then maintain more detailed knowledge on what is important. Also, requiring squad leaders to build and maintain leader books on their Soldiers and then frequently inspecting them is a way for platoon leadership to stay informed on individual Soldier issues. Leader books should be practical and kept up-to-date. Cumbersome binders that are rarely used do not keep leaders informed.

From coaching Soldiers one-on-one at the range to opportunity training and teaching classes, squad leaders execute individual training. A key part of the training management process is certifying leaders. Platoon leadership should know what its subordinates are able to train and need to develop those leaders who are not to standard. Empowering and enabling squad leaders to be masters of their trade will build a technically and tactically proficient platoon.

Platoon leadership works through squad leaders to be effective. Leadership relies on squad leaders to assist in planning, execute rehearsals, perform PCCs, interface daily with Soldiers, and effectively train the platoon. Platoon leadership must run an effective counseling program where squad leaders are coached and mentored and live by "trust but verify."

Effective Counseling at the Platoon Level

> *"Get to know and understand your Soldiers. You have to be a leader who can have a positive impact with your Soldiers. Take the time when you are conducting their initial counseling. Explain to the Soldiers what you expect from them and what they will expect from you."*
>
> — Current field artillery PSG

Counseling is the tool used by PLs and PSGs to coach and mentor their subordinates. Formal and informal counseling are important, but documentation of sessions is key to maintaining a common operational picture. Successful platoon counseling programs track performance over time, are timely, leverage both PLs and PSGs, and are documented.

Counseling is a tool that allows leaders to track a subordinate's growth and performance over time. Regular counseling allows leaders to track positive and negative performance, building an evaluation over the year. Prerecording talking points in Department of Army (DA) Form 4856, Developmental Counseling Form, makes it easier to stick to talking points especially if they are on negative performance. Having a 1SG review negative counseling before it is given ensures company-level buy-in and support and keeps leadership informed of their subordinate's actions.

PLs and PSGs use a combination of formal and informal counseling to ensure direction is timely. Leaders use informal counseling: Pulling a squad leader off the line during a down period to discuss employment of obscuration at the breach during a squad live fire to improve a squad's performance on the next iteration. Leaders use formal counseling: Reviewing a squad leader's performance at the JRTC to document performance over time on DA Form 4856 after returning to home station. A combination of formal and informal counseling allows impactful counseling that creates growth in a platoon.

For Platoon Leaders

As a PL, you are critical to the counseling process because you are the squad leader's senior rater. It can be difficult to counsel a Soldier who is older or has more experience and time in service than you. Before your session, discuss your thoughts with your PSG and prepare your points on DA Form 4856 as well as an NCO support form. Engage your junior leaders to develop plans of actions for themselves. Finally, allow your Soldiers to contribute to the success of the platoon, let them input how they would improve the platoon. Having a plan and empowering and engaging your leaders can help ease a difficult counseling session.

For Platoon Sergeants

As a PSG, you will run your platoon's counseling program. Speak with the 1SG and understand his expectations and requirements. Successful platoons run disciplined, timely, and documented counseling programs. You should review and provide input into each counseling packet as needed. Your PL will need mentoring in his requirements and expectations for counseling. Spend the time and effort here to get this right, it will pay dividends throughout your platoon.

The Platoon Leader and Platoon Sergeant Counseling Session

This counseling session can be the most difficult and is the most important session in the platoon. Use this opportunity to honestly discuss your platoon and what needs to be done to improve it. Setting joint goals and a plan of action to achieve them builds buy in. Neither the PL nor the PSG can go into this counseling session with directives. Both need to come with thoughts and expectations. Remember you either succeed or fail as a team; you need each other.

A Platoon Leader on Counseling a Platoon Sergeant

"Set a date and time that is good for the both of you, either in your office or over a meal. Make the counseling a conversation rather than you reading topics to him. Don't make the mistake of having other NCOs or Soldiers present for a counseling between the PL and PSG. It is fine to have notes or a DA Form 4856, but try to make the conversation personal and record the topics/plan of action later. Use this time to get to know your PSG, his experiences, and work out your team vision for the platoon."

— Former cavalry PL

It is important to document counseling in DA Form 4856 or a memorandum as soon as possible after the event. Informal counseling benefits from a written document after the event to amplify and clarify the points. The document also serves as an input to the evaluation and awards processes, making it easier to take care of Soldiers.

Counseling is an important tool for leaders. PLs and PSGs counsel to track performance timely to the event while leveraging each other, using documentation. Counseling sets a base for a platoon, so no matter the operational tempo or the competing priorities, it is not overlooked by effective leaders.

Engaged Leadership

"Successful junior officers and NCOs can train, take care of people, and maintain equipment equally well. You cannot be the best if you cannot do one or more of these."

— Former brigade commander

Junior officer and NCOs' training and experience prepares them to train their platoon and maintain their equipment. Just as important to platoon success is taking care of people. PLs and PSGs engage their Soldiers through discussion and by taking the time to identify stressors, understanding the readiness implications, becoming aware of their actions, and getting Soldiers the help they need when they need it.

For Platoon Leaders and Platoon Sergeants

As a leader, you will be expected to help Soldiers with any issues that affect their readiness. This will put you into Soldiers' professional and personal lives. PLs and PSGs have expressed surprise and have been unprepared for some of the situations listed below. As a leader, you will become a life coach to your Soldiers because personal problems directly impact readiness. If you encounter an issue you are unprepared for as a team, use your 1SG, XO, and commander for guidance. Another source of support are peer PLs and PSGs. Do not be afraid to learn from those who served before you.

- Death of a Soldier
- Fire in a Soldier's home
- Injury of a Soldier in training
- Death of a Soldier's family member
- Unplanned pregnancy
- Help a Soldier or spouse gain citizenship
- Extramarital affair
- Bullying/hazing (Soldiers/peers/leaders)
- Domestic abuse
- Loss of a car (unable to get to work)
- Suicidal ideation
- Suicide (Soldier or family member)
- Drug/alcohol issues
- Financial issues
- Sexual assault of a Soldier
- Theft of Army property
- NCO misconduct
- Marital problems
- Premarital counseling

PLs and PSGs should be constantly aware of their Soldiers and any stressors they may have. Soldiers often share information about themselves through counseling, peers, and their actions. Just because someone has been serving a long time does not mean that they do not have personal or discipline issues. Watch NCOs for these and get them the help they need. In addition, as an Army leader, pay attention to your partner (PL/PSG), peers, and even superiors who may require support. Leaders who are more engaged can better pick out a cry for help by a Soldier. A best practice is for leaders to engage Soldiers on their off time by having a physical presence in the barracks. Soldiers tend to share more during their off time.

Military and Life Stressors

All Soldiers at one point go through one or more of the stressors listed below. It is the job of an engaged leader to know his Soldiers, what stressors may be affecting them, and how to support them. Review this amended list from Army Regulation (AR) 600-85, The Army Substance Abuse Program (ASAP).[5] This list is not all inclusive, but is a starting point:

- Recent family death: Spouse, child, mother, or father
- Accidents: Military or civilian vehicle
- Injuries: On or off the job, long-term physical disability, Medical Readiness Boards, Soldier, or family member
- Military standards: Failure on the Army physical fitness test (APFT), difficulties with medical standards, or unable to meet uniform standards
- Suicide attempts: Actual or ideation, Soldier or family member
- Drug offenses: Positive urinalysis, indicators of drug use in barracks
- Alcohol offenses: Underage drinking, excessive or public intoxication, DUI, or enrollment in ASAP
- Traffic violations: Excessive speeding or multiple tickets
- Criminal action: Arrest on or off post
- Spouse or child abuse: Soldier on spouse/child or spouse on Soldier/child
- Financial problems: Frequent Army Emergency Relief (AER) loans or issues with credit
- Chapter elimination: Pending or actively in the process
- Disciplinary actions: Pending Article 15 of the Uniform Code of Military Justice, bar to reenlistment, or extra duty
- Major life changes: Marriage, divorce, new child, or recent permanent change of station
- Deployment: Pending or returning

Taking care of Soldiers' families and issues is often overlooked by leaders. This may seem to work in the short-term but always fails. Again, successful platoons "take care of people, and maintain equipment equally well." Once Soldier issues or concerns are overlooked by the chain of command, trust and relationships are broken, destroying platoon cohesion. The Soldier who needs to leave the field to take care of a family issue or who does not have a plan for a non-driving spouse to get to the commissary during a unit rotation at a combat training center detracts from the platoon's readiness. The PL and PSG's job as a link to the company is critical to ensuring Soldiers and families are prepared for their jobs. Leaders who are involved in welcoming and counseling their Soldiers can often identify issues before they become problems.

Once a leader identifies what is going on with a Soldier, PLs and PSGs need to be aware of how their actions affect that Soldier. Leaders who ignore problems, belittle problems, or are overly aggressive with discipline can put Soldiers into a downward spiral. For example, a PL and PSG were flippant during a suicide awareness class. Later, one of their Soldiers, who is going through a divorce because of a positive drug test, arrives late to formation and is chewed out in front of his peers. If the Soldier was contemplating suicide because of the drug and family issues, he now knows his leaders do not care and are not there to support him. He now has an additional stressor created by leadership. Contrast this with a PL and PSG who actively engage during a suicide awareness class and, when the Soldier is late, take the Soldier aside and ask what is going on during counseling. The second Soldier knows his leadership is there to support him, which, in turn, helps him build resiliency. Some of the hardest leadership involves bringing a "lost cause" back as a productive member of the platoon.

After identifying issues and understanding how their actions affect Soldiers, engaged leaders help Soldiers get the help they need. The Army has multiple programs to help Soldiers: the battalion chaplain (one-on-one help), brigade-embedded behavioral health (post-traumatic stress disorder or suicidal ideations), Army Community Services (multiple programs), the Family Advocacy Program (spouse and child abuse), ASAP (drug and alcohol issues), and military family life counselors (one-on-one counseling and financial help). A platoon-level leader may not know of all these programs, but should use the company chain of command. Additional programs, along with family resiliency, is discussed further in Chapter 3, Knowledge.

A platoon-level leader will need to take care of his Soldiers. Engaged leaders are part of the solution for their platoon and not an additional source of stress. Engaged leaders know how to identify stressors, understand how stressors affect readiness, are aware of Soldiers' actions, and know how and where to get help the Soldiers need. No one is immune to stress, and leaders can either build or destroy their platoon through their actions.

Time and Task Management for a Platoon

> *"I have seen platoon leaders who operate in chaos, they are everywhere at once, try to do it all themselves, provide no clear guidance, and do not know their own end state. These guys cannot get their eyes off the 50-meter targets and never get to the important stuff."*
>
> — Current armor PSG

PLs and PSGs manage their platoon's time and tasks. A leader will have to prioritize tasks, provide guidance, delegate duties, and communicate up the chain of command. Often, platoons are asked to do more than they feel they can do. Proper time and task management allows platoons to complete their mission.

When in the field, platoon-level leaders prioritize their tasks using the priorities of work. In garrison, there is no such model, but leaders should build one based on their commander's requirements and priorities. A way to prioritize daily tasks is through "go-home criteria" and frequent backbriefs. The leader identifies what has to be done that day versus what can be held off until the next day. At the end of the day, the leader can confirm with his squad leaders the status of tasks through a backbrief and push a situation report (SITREP) to his company leadership as needed.

PLs and PSGs receive guidance and orders from their company command team, battalion staff, and other sources. Leaders should take time to understand their mission, ask clarification questions as needed, and confirm guidance with a backbrief. Do not be afraid to ask questions; a shared understanding now will prevent conflict in the future. When platoon-level leaders brief, they should be precise and to the point, encourage questions from their platoon, and require a backbrief from their squad leaders.

Platoon-level leaders manage and delegate tasks to their squad leaders for execution. In the field, squads are task-organized and given a task and purpose. In garrison, squads should be treated the same. Knowing junior leaders' abilities allows platoon leadership to delegate the right task to the right junior leader. For delegated tasks, PLs and PSGs should include time for squad-level planning, PCIs, and backbriefs. At a minimum, the one-third, two-thirds rule used during troop-leading procedures (TLPs) should be used in garrison.

As the point of connection to the company, platoon-level leadership must understand how to communicate up and down the chain of command. A key component to effective communication is providing senior leaders with situational understanding to make decisions. A leader who has a thorough understanding of priorities and risk can speak in terms of options. Providing options in terms of priorities, "the platoon can stay at the qualification range and increase our number of experts, but we would be unable to make the company family readiness group meeting tonight," or risk, "my drivers will be tired coming off their first mission, delaying our next mission, but giving them six hours of sleep will prevent accidents," enables a senior leader to make an educated decision.

The Company Training Calendar

One way a company manages time is through the company training calendar. Once a calendar is signed by the battalion commander and posted, it is used to identify when platoons are supporting and executing company and higher events and when they have time to execute platoon internal duties and training. Platoons that plan to support their company's training calendar have an easier time prioritizing their tasks. Ensuring that Soldiers understand the training calendar and what they will be doing keeps morale high by providing predictability.

Time and task management is difficult for platoons. Platoon-level leaders can make their job easier through prioritizing tasks, providing clear guidance, delegating duties, and communicating properly to their commander. By keeping on top of their platoon's time and tasks, leaders gain more time to build their team, train, and have downtime with their platoon, raising their platoon's readiness and morale.

Notes on Mission Command

> *"Leadership time is high strung, but you need to be patient with yourself and with your subordinates. Make sure that any direction/ guidance you provide is clear and unambiguous, and if the result is not what you had hoped for, write it off as an honest mistake. There is no reason to lose patience and become irrational. People respect confidence and patience because it makes you a rational logical thinker."*
>
> — Former engineer PL

Mission command is the exercise of authority and direction by the commander using mission orders to enable disciplined initiative within the commander's intent to empower agile and adaptive leaders,[6] or simply the process of leading through trust. Company commanders issue orders and trust their platoons to execute them within their intent. PLs and PSGs must demonstrate understanding of their commander's intent and a shared understanding of the environment. The baseline of mission command is cohesive teams (discussed earlier), trust, shared understanding, initiative, and risk.

Leaders cultivate trust up and down the chain of command at all times. At the company level, backbriefs, proper reporting, and executing within the commander's intent in garrison and training builds the trust needed between command teams and platoon leadership for a training center rotation or deployment. At the platoon level, trust is built the same way. In garrison and training, platoons that empower junior leaders with intent and check them through backbriefs and reporting, build their internal trust and are able to operate more efficiently during combat. Leaders who are approachable and get to know their Soldiers in garrison are able to empower their Soldiers more in combat.

During execution, platoons need to create shared understanding at their level and with their headquarters. Providing reports to higher in accordance with the tactical standard operating procedure (TACSOP) and requiring junior leaders to keep platoon leadership updated creates understanding of how the battlefield looks. In addition to seeing the battlefield the same way, mission orders that are clear and unambiguous along with backbriefs give leaders a shared understanding of what actions a unit will take and how they will do them. This understanding of task and purpose gives leaders the ability to synchronize across their units.

Looking at squad leaders, PLs and PSGs must be comfortable being uncomfortable and not having 100 percent situational awareness. Radio issues, communication issues, and confusion reign on the battlefield and leaders at all levels need to be comfortable executing with what they know, not what they want to know.

Initiative and risk are tied together. Leaders should be empowered to take initiative but they must temper their actions with a knowledge of risk. In combat, a PL and PSG may be the senior leaders on the ground and may have to take initiative outside their assigned task to meet the commander's intent. This should always be done with discipline, remaining within the intent, and involve a report to higher on the platoon's action. Leaders who fail to remain within the intent or keep their higher headquarters informed risk breaking trust within the unit and may cause unintended effects at higher levels.

The Army's concept of mission command can cause friction and each leader approaches it differently. Plainly, mission command is the process of leading through trust. In today's operational environment, a platoon may find itself operating independently from its company and will find that a cohesive team (discussed earlier) enabled with trust, shared understanding, initiative, and a knowledge of risk allows it to operate within the mission command concept.

Endnotes

1. Army Doctrine Publication (ADP) 6-22, *Army Leadership*, 01 August 2012, page 6-22.

2. Lopez, C. Todd. "Army Chief of Staff Urges Soldiers to Take Responsibility for Unit, Individual Readiness," 11 October 2017. Available online at https://www.army.mil/article/195130/army_chief_of_staff_urges_soldiers_to_take_responsibility_for_unit_individual_readiness.

3. Safer, Scott. "Building a Cohesive Team." in *Company Command,* April 2013, page 69. Available online at https://www.usma.edu/caldol/siteassets/armymagazine/docs/2013/CC_ARMY_(Apr2013)_Cohesive_Team.pdf.

4. 1LT Young, Brock. "What NOT to Do as a Platoon Leader," in *Company Command,* December 2013, page 53. Available online at https://www.usma.edu/caldol/siteassets/armymagazine/docs/2013/CC_ARMY_(Dec2013)_What_NOT_to_do.pdf.

5. AR 600-85, The Army Substance Abuse Program, 28 November 2016.

6. ADP 6-0, *Mission Command*, 17 May 2012, page 1.

Chapter 2

Platoon Training

Overview

Platoon leaders (PLs) and platoon sergeants (PSGs) train Soldiers on individual tasks to support their company's collective tasks and mission essential task list (METL). After deciding what to train, leaders develop training plans for Soldiers to master their individual tasks. Successful PLs and PSGs know what resources are available and leverage them to enhance unit training.

This chapter discusses training management at the platoon level, what to train, opportunity training, sergeant's time training (STT), preparing your first range, and training resources.

Training Management at the Platoon Level

> *"The platoon would have benefited if the platoon sergeant and myself had built the standard for what products were needed for the training schedule. We would build these products ... to T+12 for the first three months when I was platoon leader. However, as T+13 came in and the commander's guidance was given, the squad leaders and team leaders should be involved in building those training schedules/products. This would have elicited their buy-in (since they were included in the planning effort) and they would have training products to reference (including what information the products need in order to meet the standard)."*
>
> — Former combat arms PL

Training management at the platoon level is designed to train individual Soldiers to support higher-level collective tasks. PLs and PSGs must use their knowledge and experience to look at the company training calendar, identify what tasks support company events and what tasks the platoon is deficient in, and design a training path to prepare their Soldiers.

Companies plan and execute training using the T-week concept. The T-week concept is a 13-week calendar that ensures companies properly plan, resource, prepare for, and execute training. Platoons are expected to support the company and plan and brief within the T-week calendar. PLs and PSGs should use the less formal eight-step training model to plan and resource individual training within their commander's training calendar.

Companies and platoons use troop-leading procedures (TLPs) to plan training. In addition to the TLPs, platoons and squads use the eight-step training model to identify and take critical steps needed to plan and prepare for training events. The eight-step training model provides a way to continually improve, from planning to preparing, executing, assessing, and then planning for the next event (see Figure 2-1).

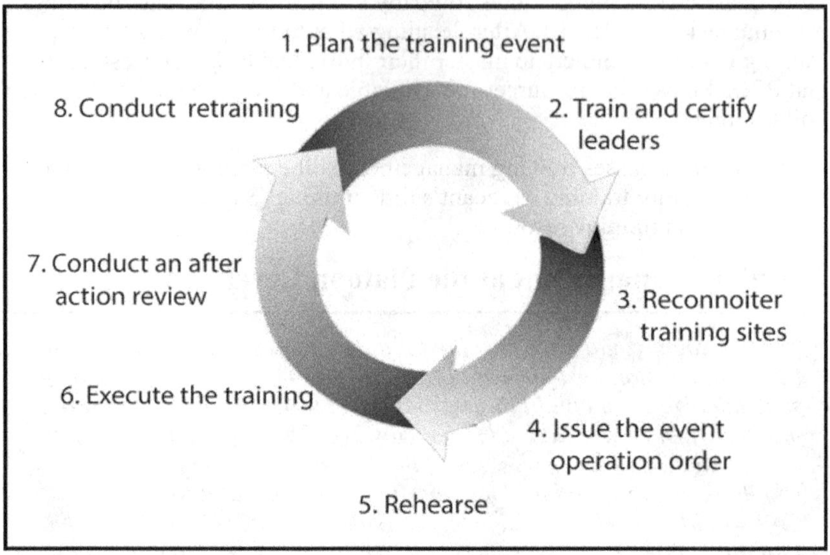

Figure 2-1. Eight-step training model[1]

The company uses the weekly training meeting to plan and assess training. Platoons input the current training status and plans based on the T-week concept. This is the focal point of the training calendar. It gives PLs and PSGs a chance to brief their training and ensure it nests with the company training path.

Platoon-level leaders track their training individually by team and squad using a platoon-training tracker or Excel spreadsheet (see Table 2-1). Tracking Soldiers through events keeps leaders on the pulse of their unit and will help determine what needs to be trained. Keeping this information also feeds the company when the data is needed for higher briefings and meetings. This data should be in a leader's smartbook (see Appendix A, Platoon Smartbook).

Table 2-1. Example platoon training tracker

Name	APFT	APFT Date	12 Mile	Individual Weapon Qualification	CLS	Driver's License
SSG C.	264	22 Jun	11 AUG	M4 (11/19)	APR	Y
SGT S.	247	10 Aug	22 JUL	M4 (11/19)	APR	Y
PV2 R.	211	29 Apr	4 SEP	M4 (7/9)	APR	Y
PVT R.	299	11 May	15 MAR	M4 (11/19)		N
SPC G.	263	4 Aug	24 NOV	M249 (8/11)	APR	Y

APFT Army physical fitness test
CLS combat life saver
PVT private
PV2 private 2nd class
SGT sergeant
SPC specialist
SSG staff sergeant

After seeing how the platoon fits into the company training calendar and having knowledge of where it stands, platoon leadership identifies white space on the company calendar and develops training plans to prepare Soldiers individually and collectively for higher-level training. These plans are briefed to and approved by company leadership at the weekly company training meeting.

Platoons manage training at the platoon level by understanding how company training management works, providing input during the company training meeting, tracking the platoon, and developing training that supports higher-level collective tasks. This is done in support of the company commander and through dialogue between the platoon and company leadership.

Training

> *"I just spent all day reviewing Army Training Network (ATN) and teaching my platoon leaders how to do a METL crosswalk to identify training tasks. Last week when I visited my platoons in the field, I found them training on what they did during the deployment to Afghanistan. That's great, but we go to the Joint Readiness Training Center (JRTC) in a couple months, so I had to reorient my platoons from stability operations to decisive action."*
>
> — Current company commander talking to a peer

The first step for training at the platoon level is to determine what to train on. Leaders and units are restricted in their tactical-task training time due to competing priorities such as taskings, mandatory 350-1 training, maintenance, and other requirements. To make the most efficient use of training time, platoons should research their company's METL, identify individual and collective tasks that input into the METL at the platoon level, decide what to train on, and then prepare training plans to meet that mission essential task (MET).

Leaders should know and use ATN (online at https://atn.army.mil [authorized users only, CAC login required]) to identify what to train on. Once on ATN, the Combined Arms Training Strategies (CATS) lets users look up their company's METs and the supporting collective and individual tasks (see Figure 2-2).

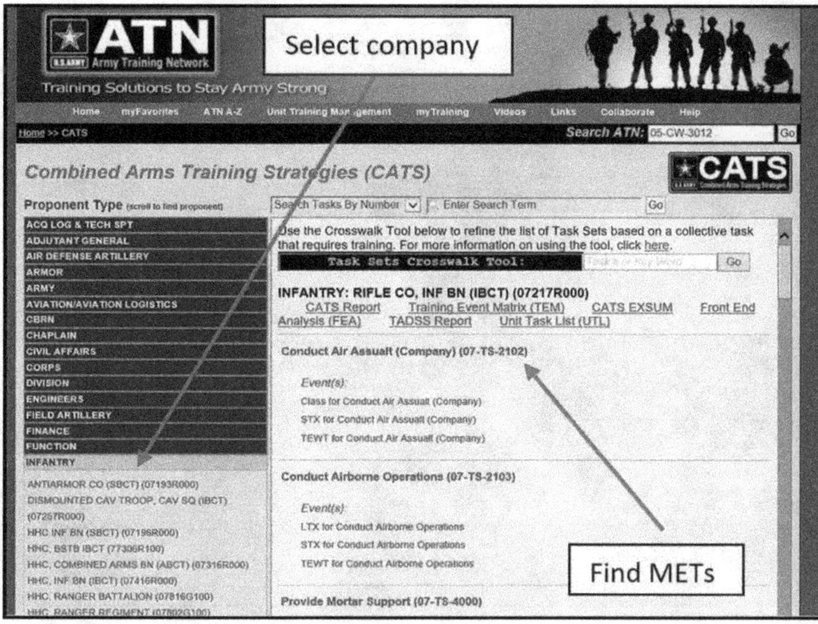

Fig 2-2. CATS tool site

For example, if an infantry brigade combat team rifle company is planning a situational training exercise (STX) for platoons in an urban area, a quick search reveals a collective task focused on conducting an attack in an urban area (see Figure 2-3). Clicking on this collective task shows the Training and Evaluation Outline (T&EO). At the bottom of the T&EO is a list of supporting individual tasks which includes “Enter a Building During an Urban Operation.” Searching for that individual task will then give leaders a summary with performance steps and “Go/No Go” performance measures.

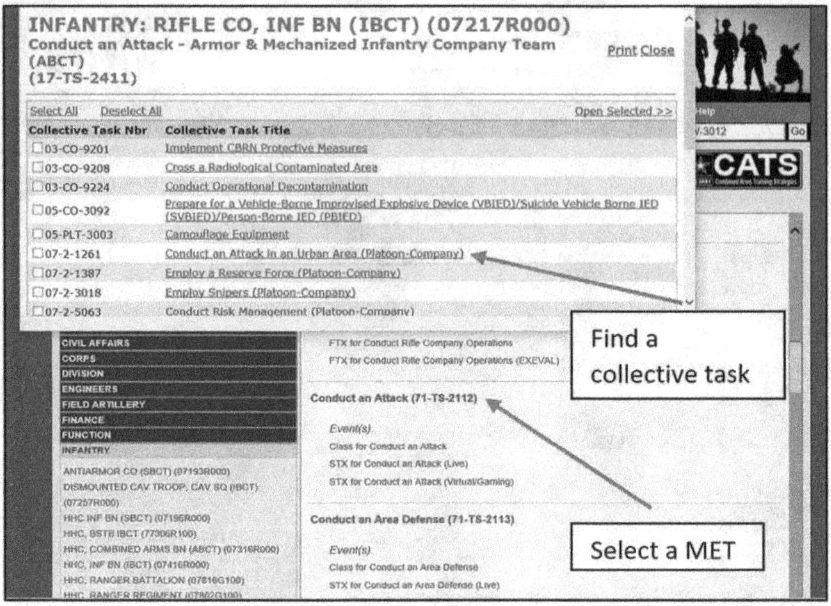

Fig 2-3. CATS collective tasks

Leaders must understand their commander's intent when deciding what tasks to train on. For this example, there are also collective tasks for breaching a mined wire obstacle. If the intent of the company STX is to validate the ability of a platoon to seize a building during an urban operation, focusing on mined wire obstacles may not lead to the culminating company event even though it is within the same MET. Knowing the commander's training path and intent will allow leaders to complement it.

For Platoon Leaders

As a PL, it is your job to decide what to train and plan training. You are also the point of contact between your platoon and company leadership through the training meeting. As you identify white space on the calendar and decide with your PSG and squad leaders what needs to be done at the platoon level, be sure to give your commander a backbrief. What to train on is always a conversation between PLs and commanders. Maintaining an open and constant line of communication is key for PLs.

Identifying what to train on is a critical step of the training process. Leaders who do not take time here plan and execute non-relevant training or waste Soldiers' time. To execute properly, platoon-level leaders must research their company's METL, identify which individual and collective tasks support particular METs, decide on training, and then prepare training plans to meet the METs. After identifying what to train, platoon-level leaders can use STT and opportunity training to prepare their units for their mission.

Opportunity Training

> *"Opportunity training is key; following the program of instruction is good, but providing more training outside of the prescribed calendar pays huge dividends."*
>
> — Outgoing PL

Opportunity or "hip-pocket" training focuses at the individual level. It is training a unit can use when it experiences inactive periods during scheduled training. Ideally, opportunity training should take 15 to 30 minutes, giving leaders flexibility to insert it when needed.[2] Opportunity training maximizes training time and prevents lost training opportunities.

Opportunity training should focus on the basics and nest with the platoon's training path. This should be a collaborative discussion with the squad leaders to decide the tasks on which to train. Each squad may be different. Radio operations, individual- and small-unit movement techniques, communications, or fire control measures are all examples of tasks that may nest within a platoon's train-up for a STX lane.

Opportunity training should be planned using the eight-step training model. When selecting what to train on, leaders should look at collective tasks in ATN and identify individual tasks. Using T&EOs from ATN provides leaders with task, conditions, and standards for training and helps leaders identify the required training resources. Certifying leaders remains a key step in the planning process to ensure quality training. Another key resource is Soldier Training Publication (STP) 21-1-Soldier's Manual of Common Tasks (SMCT), *Warrior Skills Level 1* (October 2006), which lays out the Army's key individual tasks by shoot, move, communicate, and survive. List opportunity training tasks on the training schedule to remind leaders what tasks they agreed to train on so they can prepare to execute.

Some platoons have difficulty finding time for opportunity training, but there is often time available that leaders tend to overlook. For example, why does the post services road march have to be an administrative move? It can easily be turned into a tactical move where the platoon can practice coils, herringbones, react to contact, and recovery drills. This would allow the platoon to not only test its equipment, but also improve its tactical skills without using any additional time.

Opportunity training is key to ensuring units sustain training and are prepared for collective tasks. Platoon-level leaders should develop a training plan that nests their training, focuses on the basics, and is planned with the eight-step training model. Platoon-level leaders should then backbrief their company leadership to get buy-in from their leaders. Having squad leaders prepare and maintain smartbooks with task, conditions, standards, and equipment needed enables platoons to execute and track training.

Sergeant's Time Training

> *"An effective STT program is not a "dog and pony show." If your junior noncommissioned officers (NCOs) have to concern themselves with things like laminated butcher block paper, a welcome committee for visitors, and risk assessment worksheets, they will spend more time focusing on those items than the task for which they are training."*
>
> — Former battalion command sergeant major

STT is a battle-rhythm event planned and executed at the platoon and below level where NCOs train key individual and collective tasks. STT tasks should be selected and planned, each having a task, condition, and standard.

Squad leaders are the key to a strong STT program. Direction in what to train on may come from the company or platoon level, but squad leaders will take that direction and turn it into training plans and instruction. As junior leaders build their training plans and backbrief platoon leadership, they will gain confidence in their training. This confidence will result in squad leaders who are sure of their skills in leading their squad, and platoon leadership that know how its subordinates will act in certain situations.

For Platoon Sergeants

As the senior NCO, it is tempting for you to take personal charge and run with STT. This will hurt your platoon for two reasons. First, as a PSG you now have additional responsibilities to the company that will drag you away from training. You do not have the time in the day to do both. Second, it is your responsibility to build your junior leaders. Giving your junior leaders the opportunity to learn and teach will help them and the Army better than you teaching.

STT is designed to separate Soldiers from the administrative responsibilities at the company for a given amount of time. Isolating STT protects it from training distractions such as reports, taskings, or medical appointments. Platoon-level leaders should protect this time as much as possible. An easy way to protect STT is to ensure it is on the company training calendar and to send squads away from the company to train in a designated training area or other location separating them physically from the company.

STT allows leaders to cross-train their unit as needed. STT tasks should nest with the company training path as noted above, but junior leaders are given some additional flexibility to identify and train on needed tasks. For example, a unit training for a route clearance mission may plan a STT on recovery tasks with a wrecker. Although not specifically related to route clearance, having more Soldiers in the platoon knowledgeable on recovery will make the platoon more effective.

STT gives squad leaders confidence and buy-in, separates Soldiers from administrative responsibilities, and allows leaders to cross-train as needed. STT is a critical part of a platoon's training plan and it should be planned, briefed, and approved just as any other training.

Preparing Your First Range

> *"Our PLs have a difficult time planning training. Most cannot seem to wrap their heads around how to identify what to train, find land, figure out what ammunition they need, and plan a range. They expect everything to be top down and set up for them based on gunnery and external requirements. Our leaders need to be proactive, planning from the bottom up to be successful."*
>
> — Armor company commander

PLs and PSGs often act as the officer in charge (OIC), noncommissioned officer in charge (NCOIC), or range safety officer (RSO) during platoon and company training. This job may be the first time a platoon-level leader plans and executes a training event, which can be a source of confusion and struggle for new leaders. Leaders may be expected to brief based on the T-week model during company training meetings. Platoon-level leaders use the eight-step training model and TLPs to plan their event. Below is a way to plan a range using TLPs.

1. Receive the mission

There are multiple ways to receive the mission to plan and execute a range. Critical during this step is determining the training audience and the commander's intent and end state for the event. Platoon-level leaders should confirm what they know using a backbrief to their commander, showing a thorough understanding of the mission before starting to plan. The company executive officer (XO) is a key resource during this phase. The XO can often provide historical data, expectations, templates, and other assistance needed during the planning phases.

2. Issue the warning order (WARNORD)

Planning is a collaborative event. The OIC will lead, but needs to assemble his NCOIC, RSO, and other key leaders as soon as possible and provide them a WARNORD. The range's date and time should be on the company training calendar and distributed to junior leaders to allow them to start planning in parallel.

3. Make a tentative plan

Making a tentative plan starts step one of the eight-step training model: Plan the training event. Before determining the details, leaders should gather the tools needed to plan. OICs and NCOICs need to determine which field manual contains the qualification standards for the weapon system to be trained, access the Army's Standards in Training Commission (STRAC) on the Army Training Support Center's (ATSC's) website (authorized users only, CAC login required) to determine the authorized ammunition, review the unit standard operating procedure (SOP), collect information from the local range branch, print any relevant T&EOs, and gather any other applicable documents. After gathering their tools, the OIC, NCOIC, and RSO develop a tentative plan in collaboration with each other, squad leaders, and any other relevant stakeholders.

4. Initiate movement

As the OIC, NCOIC, and RSO build their plan, junior leaders should be empowered to prepare. Squad leaders can do layouts of key equipment or lead preliminary marksmanship instruction (PMI) as part of STT.

Critical during the initiate movement step is step two of the eight-step training model: Train and certify leaders. This should be a planned and briefed event during the company training meeting that ensures trainers are ready to lead training.

5. Conduct reconnaissance

Conduct reconnaissance encompasses step three of the eight-step training model: Reconnoiter training sites. It is invaluable to get on the ground during mission planning. Simple tasks such as confirming the number and type of lanes for firing or the location of the ammunition point, water point, casualty collection point, concurrent training site, retraining site, and other key locations can be seen on the ground. Oftentimes, coordination with range control must be done prior to a reconnaissance, so this should be planned early. This not only allows permission to be on the range, it also gives leadership the opportunity to see the full capabilities of the training site.

6. Complete the plan

Complete the plan ends step one of the eight-step training model. Here, the tentative plan is confirmed and modified based on the reconnaissance. The RSO builds the risk assessment with input from the OIC and NCOIC. Risk assessments should not be reproduced from previous ranges and should include any risks from all phases of the range. During this step, OICs brief their company and battalion commanders to obtain their approval and sign the risk assessment.

Part of completing the plan is submitting it to range control in accordance with the local SOP. Oftentimes, a concept of operations (CONOPS) brief and a signed risk assessment are due to range control at a set time before the range can lock in land. Be aware of timelines out of the control of the company.

7. Issue the order

Issue the order encompasses step four of the eight-step training model: Issue the event operation order (OPORD). During this step, the order is issued to subordinates who will facilitate the range but also to any other platoons or companies who may attend. The preferred method to issuing the order is through a five-paragraph OPORD that communicates all aspects of the range. The OIC may have already built a CONOPS brief for the company and battalion commanders, which can be used to enhance the OPORD during briefing.

8. Supervise

During the supervise step, leaders execute steps five through eight of the eight-step training model: Rehearse, execute the training, conduct an after action review (AAR), and conduct retraining.

Range execution starts with rehearsals and PCIs and moves through occupation of the range and firing. Leaders can execute multiple types of rehearsals, but getting key leaders on the range, if possible, is preferable. Rehearsing the casualty evacuation (CASEVAC)/medical evacuation (MEDEVAC) plan using the actual personnel, medics, and vehicles along the full route from the range to the hospital allows the OIC, NCOIC, and RSO to confirm their ability in executing a CASEVAC if needed. PCIs should include any key platoon equipment needed for the range.

During execution, the OIC and RSO should keep a copy of the risk assessment on them to continue assessing risk and implementing controls as needed. The OIC and NCOIC are often required to send situation reports (SITREPs) and other reports to higher during execution.

After the training event is complete, a thorough AAR should be conducted of the non-tactical administration of the range and of any tactical tasks evaluated using a T&EO. The administrative AAR allows the OIC, NCOIC, and RSO to improve their planning and execution for the next range. The tactical AAR will help junior leaders determine what needs to be retrained during STT and future ranges. Both AARs should be submitted to the battalion through the chain of command to share lessons learned and best practices throughout the unit.

A Story of Two Ranges

Alpha Company

PVT Parker sat down on the bleachers. All he could think about was the Call of Modern Warfare game he and his roommate were going to play that night. It already felt like a long day. His platoon skipped physical training, drew weapons from the arms room from 0800 to 0900, loaded up on buses at 0930, and arrived at the range around 1000. After a quick safety brief, he had zeroed his rifle quickly but had some issues on the qualification range. He was sent to retraining and SSG Hernandez reprimanded him about not taking the PMI seriously. PVT Parker did not understand; it was not his fault he and the rest of A Company spent Monday standing around in the motor pool after the PMI was completed.

It was 1400 now and PVT Parker qualified on the second time through. As he sat on the bleachers, he dug into his meal, ready-to-eat (MRE) and took out his phone. It would be another couple hours before the bus came at 1600 to pick up his platoon.

Bravo Company

SPC Babin of 2nd Platoon took a knee as the platoon halted the tactical foot march 1 kilometer from the range. It looked as if the platoon was starting to conduct a linear danger-area crossing of the road ahead to enter the woodline near the rifle range and go into patrol base operations. He shifted the weight on his rucksack onto his hips to relieve pressure on his shoulders. It was 1200 and it already felt like the platoon had been moving all day. Earlier that morning, his team leader inspected his kit, they drew weapons, and the entire company departed the company area at 0700 and walked 12 kilometers to the range. The 1st Platoon began movement first as they were tasked with running the range. The 2nd Platoon would qualify first, while 3rd Platoon conducted patrol base operations and local patrolling. The platoons would then rotate duties to ensure all units were trained in running a range, qualifying with weapons, and patrolling operations.

Bravo Company (continued)

Once 2nd Platoon got to the patrol base, SPC Babin's platoon established security and sectors of fire. When the platoon leader and platoon sergeant were satisfied with the patrol base, the platoon conducted a combat patrol to the company command post to receive a range orientation and safety brief. SPC Babin could see his roommate, the commander's driver, inside the command post taking notes on a whiteboard and updating the locations of the platoons on a map. The RTO in the command post sent a message over frequency modulation (FM) to the battalion staff duty that Bravo Company had arrived at the training area.

The previous 2nd Platoon leader, now the XO, and supply sergeant arrived with hot chow for lunch. While the Soldiers ate, the nuclear-biological-chemical NCO gave a quick class to the leaders on field sanitation. Following the meal, 2nd Platoon was moved back across the road to an adjacent training area. The previous day, during the OPORD brief, SPC Babin's platoon leader talked about setting up a patrol base and there would be a night vision goggle (NVG) class that night. They would then ruck back into the company bay in the morning under limited visibility using their NVGs. SPC Babin was excited; he loved being out in the night and the feeling it gave him of being a Soldier in defense of the nation. This was why he joined the Army.

After lunch, SPC Babin's team was third in the order for zero and qualification and SGT Smith, his team leader, had pulled them in to go over some additional PMI during the wait. It paid off. With SGT Smith behind him coaching, SPC Babin had qualified expert for the first time. The company commander and first sergeant had directed that while 1st Platoon had responsibility to run the range, it was the responsibility of a platoon's leadership to ensure individual Soldiers received coaching from their team leaders during marksmanship training.

The next morning during weapon recovery, the company hosted an AAR. In the AAR, the company master driver recommended that at the next range or large company training event, Bravo Company should incorporate tactical vehicles. The company could start off with driver training, transport the company to a tactical vehicle dismount location, and patrol the rest of the way to the range. This would add maintenance, driver training, load planning, and route planning and reconnaissance to the training.

Which range do you want to run? It is your mission to prepare your platoon for combat, take every opportunity you have to do so.

Training Resources

PLs and PSGs should know the resources that exist to support training. There are multiple types of simulations and training aids that can enhance platoon training. Below are some key training enablers:

Training support center (TSC). The TSC on each post provides training aids, devices, simulations, and simulators (TADSS) for training. Normally, platoon sergeants are on the company's signature card and can sign out training aids for use. Using TADSS helps provide realistic training for the platoon.

Home-Station Instrumentation Training System (HITS). HITS is designed to work with the Instrumentable Multiple Integrated Laser Engagement System (IMILES). When combined, HITS gives units a powerful tool to collect data from live training events to include location, real-time audio/video, and the effect of simulated battlefield effects. HITS should be used when units train force-on-force during STXs/field training exercises (FTXs) and is supported out of TSCs.

Range control. Range control is a resource for leaders planning ranges. They can often share previous range packets and help refine static or live-fire range plans to make sure they are realistic and safe, and will get approved. When assigned to run a range, one of the first places a leader should check is with the installation range control.

Engagement skills trainer (EST). EST is a training platform that provides simulated weapons and virtual feedback on a screen. EST should be part of every PMI to give Soldiers virtual repetitions before a range is executed.

Virtual Battle Space 2 (VBS2). VBS2 is a digital video game-based training platform that provides a way for platoons to execute training virtually without needing land, vehicles, or equipment. Like EST, VBS2 can be used as part of a train-up, giving a platoon virtual repetitions at a task before executing the task live.

Mission training complex. Each installation's mission training complex provides an array of training opportunities. Using the mission training complex staff can help train and certify leaders on key radio and mission command systems. The mission training complex also provides command post and digital exercises to stress headquarters functions.

Counter-Improvised Explosive Device Integration Cell (CI2C). Most Forces Command (FORSCOM) installations have a team of civilians who run their CI2C. They maintain currency on the improvised explosive device (IED) threat and can help provide realistic theater-specific counter IED training to platoons. Deploying units that will face an IED threat should take ample advantage of their CI2C.

Center for Army Lessons Learned (CALL). CALL provides multiple handbooks on trends and best practices throughout the Army. The CALL website at https://call2.army.mil/Login.aspx (authorized users only, CAC logon required) can be used to research trends at the combat training centers, read lessons from deployed units, and order hard copies of publications at no cost. If unsure where to start, use the request for information section to engage directly with analysts.

Army Training Network (ATN). Use ATN when planning all training events. The ATN website at https://atn.army.mil (authorized users only, CAC logon required) enables leaders to identify tasks related to their METL; provides information on Army Regulation (AR) 350-1, Army Training and Leader Development (10 DEC 2017); and can provide digital training to junior leaders on how to plan and execute a training event.

Endnotes

1. CALL 17-08, *Home Station Training Handbook*, 29 MAR 2017, page 29.
2. Field Manual 7-0, *Train to Win in a Complex World*, 05 OCT 2016.

Chapter 3

Knowledge

Overview

Platoon leaders (PLs) and platoon sergeants (PSGs) are often the most trained, experienced, and educated Soldiers in the platoon. They are responsible for training and educating their Soldiers on tactical tasks and Army programs such as the Command Supply Discipline Program (CSDP). Leaders often rely on what is taught in the officer leadership and noncommissioned officer (NCO) professional development system schools. This is a solid basis. However, successful leaders continue to educate themselves to keep abreast of changes throughout their career.

This chapter discusses command supply discipline, the company maintenance system, platoon cohesion and discipline, and family readiness programs.

Command Supply Discipline

> "*My first experience with property was as an assistant S-2, I had to sign for a piece of equipment that I did not know what it was nor what it did. I never got out the fielding documents or technical manual (TM) to verify that all of the subcomponents were present when I conducted my lackluster inspection when signing for the equipment. When I was on my way out, the next individual signed for the equipment the same way. To this day I do not know if all of the parts were actually present or not. Day one as a platoon leader, I knew I would not make the same mistake twice.*"
>
> — Current military intelligence company PL

Property accountability is a hallmark of a disciplined platoon. Most PLs sign for thousands of dollars of equipment they need in order to execute their mission. Platoons with effective property accountability support the company Command Supply Discipline Program (CSDP), execute inventories, sign equipment to the user level, maintain accountability in garrison and the field, and maintain a detailed property book. Failure to properly account for equipment can be a costly or even career-ending failure.

For Platoon Sergeants

Many of the requirements for property fall onto your PL because of regulation. That said, your PL will need help and guidance from you to be successful. Be there during inventories to make sure they are done right. This will also give you an opportunity to check equipment for serviceability and see how organized your squad leaders are. Hold your squad leaders accountable during counseling to their support of your PL's program. Finally, own your platoon's sensitive items when in the field. Have a correct master authorization list (MAL) and ensure squad leaders check and report their status based on the battle rhythm. An active PSG helps share the load and ensures your platoon maintains a disciplined property accountability program.

A platoon CSDP is a reflection of a company CSDP. Company commanders have various requirements from the brigade property book officer for signing their property book and cyclic sensitive-item, and command inventories. The company's requirements will drive how the commander develops and executes his CSDP. A platoon should stand ready to support the company's program with layouts for inventories and records of basic issue item shortages. Inventories and layouts should be on the company training calendar to protect them from unscheduled events. Most commanders ask PLs to review and sign their property book monthly and notify the supply sergeant and executive officer (XO) of any discrepancies in a timely manner.

Platoons lay out equipment for multiple types of inventories such as change of command, cyclic, and pre- and post-field exercises. Layouts should be executed using the most recent TM. TMs can be found on the electronic technical manuals (ETM) application on the Logistics Support Activity (LOGSA) website at https://liw.logsa.army.mil (authorized users only, CAC logon required). Be sure to request access to download relevant publications. Like items should be done at the same time and all sub hand-receipt holders should be available. Any deficiencies should be compared to the last component hand receipts and discrepancies annotated and reported to company leadership. During the first layout, ensure all platoon equipment is marked with a stencil or paint marker denoting the platoon.

A Platoon Leader's First Inventory

A platoon leader's first inventory is one of the first opportunities for a PL and PSG to work together. As you work together to plan and execute the inventory, discuss standards and decide on the expectations of each other. Ensure you have the needed documents, equipment is laid out by the TM, sub hand-receipt holders are available to sign for the equipment, and platoon equipment is properly marked.

"*I remember building my component hand receipt before inventories and placing each of the hand receipts in its own plastic sheet in a huge binder. Terrible mistake. The inventories were in the middle of the winter, we were outside, and taking each [hand receipt] out of the plastic sheet became a mess. Sheets flew everywhere, and they didn't match the TM. Best to have an updated TM for each individual end item and go down the list, marking what is there and isn't. The binder was a good final copy of what I wanted my hand receipt to look like, not a good working copy. The TMs would have been a good working copy, where I would update the hand receipt later in the office.*"

— Former PL

"*When signing for your platoon equipment, lay out the equipment by the TM. Check the equipment present (reality) versus equipment reflected on the component listing (ideal). Mark all PLT equipment with a paint marker, stencil, etc. Like items can easily get mixed up with a sister platoon. Properly sub hand receipt down to your NCOs.*"

— Outgoing PL to an incoming PL

Platoon-level leaders are responsible for signing all equipment down to the user level. This creates accountability ("I am responsible for my stuff") and ownership ("this stuff is mine"). Signing equipment down to the user is critical because it prevents a leader from having to pay for equipment. Also, the physical act of signing has more impact than a verbal order. PLs maintain both sub and component hand receipts for their equipment down to the user level. A way to further emphasize this is to add it to squad leader counseling to ensure junior leaders understand their responsibilities as property owners.

Property accountability is a garrison and field requirement. Property should be inventoried prior to going to the field to assess serviceability. The same applies as a platoon comes out of the field. Precombat inspections (PCIs) can accomplish this, ensuring the platoon has the needed equipment to execute its mission.

A critical aspect of field property accountability is sensitive-items accountability. Platoon-level leaders maintain a correct master authorization list (MAL) of weapons, night vision goggles, radios, etc. Squad leaders should be required to do the same. The MAL should be checked at least twice a day or according to the standard operating procedure (SOP). PLs and PSGs are responsible for tracking sensitive items.

Leaders maintain a property book to keep accountability of their equipment. At a minimum, it should include relevant TMs, sub and component hand receipts, and shortage annexes. Any turn-in documents or long-term hand receipts to other platoons should also be included. At times, leaders include pictures of hard-to-identify items. PLs should require squad leaders to do the same. Squad leaders' books should be inspected often for completeness.

Maintaining a solid property accountability program at the platoon level will prevent PLs and squad leaders from paying for lost equipment, keeps their equipment ready for combat, and allows platoon-level leaders to focus more on training.

For Platoon Leaders

One of your first duties as the new PL is to inventory and sign for your equipment. The way you conduct the inventory tells others what type of leader you are. Are you prepared? Do you hold people accountable? Are you organized? Do you do the hard right or do you take shortcuts? Do you adhere to standards? Getting it right sets you up for success during your leadership time. The bottom line is, this can cost you money or get you fired.

- Only sign for what you can see and touch.
- Sign all equipment down to the user and ensure it is properly sub hand receipted.
- During your first inventory, take pictures of hard-to-identify items and ensure pilferable items are marked with a stencil or paint marker.
- Execute proper inventories
- Maintain a solid property book for platoon equipment with relevant TMs, sub and component hand receipts, and shortage annexes.
- Do not take short cuts.

Platoon-Level Maintenance

"*The biggest thing that I expect from a platoon leader and sergeant is knowing the status of all of their equipment. A spreadsheet that lists every vehicle and any trailer, radio, or Duke associated with it works well. When something goes down, they should be able to say why it was down and what the expected outcome will be (replace or repair) and when the part will come in.*"

— A current forward support company commander

Platoons are asked to execute multiple types of missions, sometimes on a short timeline. It is important that a platoon maintains equipment readiness of their weapons, radios, vehicles, and other equipment. Equipment readiness is as important as personnel and training readiness.

Platoon-level leaders should complete a Department of Army (DA) Form 5988-E, Equipment Maintenance and Inspection Worksheet; plan for and supervise maintenance; and maintain equipment in the field. Maintenance and repairs are tracked on DA Form 5988-E at the platoon level. The forms are printed from the Global Combat Support System-Army (GCSS-A). The ability to read and understand a DA Form 5988-E is critical to a leader's ability to execute platoon maintenance. A properly completed DA Form 5988-E gives leaders the ability to understand their equipment's status during repairs.

When reviewing a DA Form 5988-E, a leader should first review the administrative data. The upper portion of the form lays out the equipment type, bumper number, National Stock Number (NSN), serial number, and the current mileage reading for the equipment. DA Form 5988-E also includes the relevant publication numbers for technical manuals needed for preventive maintenance checks and services (PMCS). After confirming the administrative data, leaders should review the equipment's service due data, which lays out the next service due date. The date should be on the training calendar and deconflicted with any training (see Figure 3-1).

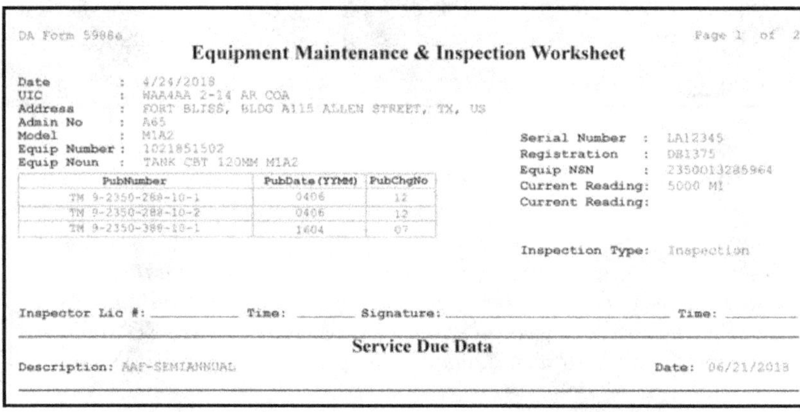
DA Form 5988e — Page 1 of 2

Equipment Maintenance & Inspection Worksheet

Date : 4/24/2018
UIC : WAA4AA 2-14 AR COA
Address : FORT BLISS, BLDG A115 ALLEN STREET, TX, US
Admin No : A65
Model : M1A2
Equip Number : 1021851502
Equip Noun : TANK CBT 120MM M1A2

PubNumber	PubDate (YYMM)	PubChgNo
TM 9-2350-288-10-1	0406	12
TM 9-2350-288-10-2	0406	12
TM 9-2350-388-10-1	1604	07

Serial Number : LA12345
Registration : DB1375
Equip NSN : 2350013286964
Current Reading: 5000 MI
Current Reading:

Inspection Type: Inspection

Inspector Lic #: ________ Time: ______ Signature: ______________ Time: ______

Service Due Data

Description: AAF-SEMIANNUAL   Date: 06/21/2018

Figure 3-1. Administrative data on a DA Form 5988-E[1]

The historical faults and parts requested section allows leaders to assess the status of their equipment (see Figure 3-2). This section is where any faults and their technical status are reviewed. Deadlined equipment cannot be dispatched without a commander's exception. Equipment with shortcomings is important to note, as it may limit a platoon's operation. The XO should be notified of any differences between the actual status and the DA Form 5988-E status.

EQUIPMENT TECHNICAL STATUS
- X Deadlined
- Circle X - Approved by CDR for Limited Operations
- Dash - Inspection
- Diagonal - Shortcoming (Notification)
- Administrative Deadline
- Equipment Status Changed

Figure 3-2. 5988-E equipment status symbols[2]

Faults should have a work-order number and a relevant work code attached. Faults that do not have a work code often have not been verified by maintenance personnel. Platoon leadership should work closely with the XO and motor sergeant to validate and update faults. The following work codes show the status of the repair work:

Work Codes[3]

0 – Begin non-mission capable (NMC) time

1 – Awaiting deadlining NMC parts

5 – Scheduled services

6 – Re-inspection

8 – Rework, return to shop

9 – Begin in-transit time

A – Awaiting initial inspection

B – In shop

C – Awaiting shop

I – In shop awaiting non-NMC parts

J – In shop awaiting NMC parts

K – Awaiting NMC parts

R – Awaiting pickup

S – Closed-completed by the maintenance activity

U – Picked up (must be closed first)

Once parts are ordered against a fault, they are tracked on DA Form 5988-E by NSN and the date the part was requested. Leaders need to be aware of the priority code (02 – five-day turnaround, 05 – eight-day turnaround, and 12 – 30-day turnaround) and request a change to the priority through the XO as needed.

After reviewing the current fault section, operators complete the PMCS and fill in the back with any additional faults. Faults should be listed by line item from the technical manual and include a "/" for shortcomings or an "X" for deadline fault per the manual. Most units require a mechanic to confirm a fault before it is input onto DA Form 5988-E. PLs and PSGs need to confirm any faults with the motor sergeant to ensure they are validated and input into the system.

Platoon-level leaders incorporate maintenance into their planning. Maintenance time should be on the company training calendar and usually designated for "motorpool Mondays." However, this time is not enough as maintenance is a daily requirement. Faults identified on Monday have to be followed up. Parts arriving to repair broken equipment need to be installed within the week. PLs and PSGs should protect this time to allow Soldiers to focus on their vehicles and equipment. In addition to protecting time, platoon leadership must ensure DA Form 5988-E and technical manuals are on-hand to allow Soldiers time to properly execute maintenance. Finally, maintenance should be personally led. There are multiple competing demands for PL and PSG's time, but a leader's presence speaks to the platoon's priorities. Leadership presence creates a culture of maintenance within the platoon.

Maintenance must happen in the field. Before, during, and after PMCS give operators the ability to ensure the readiness of their vehicle. Vehicle and weapon maintenance should be planned into any patrol. Performing after-use PMCS of vehicles in a vehicle patrol base is as critical as daily weapon maintenance in a dismounted patrol base and should be planned as part of the platoon's priorities of work.

Platoon Cohesion and Discipline

> *"Being a leader of troops is a privilege and leaders must take full advantage of the opportunity. Leaders must always maintain good order themselves, so that they may lead by example the Soldiers they are in charge of. Leaders must also be consistent on all Army standards throughout their formation. Maintaining good order and discipline and being fair and impartial when recommending both rewards and punishment for their Soldiers builds trust and maintains morale in a platoon."*
>
> — A field artillery first sergeant (1SG)

Part of building cohesion and discipline within a platoon is creating and enforcing high standards. High standards help create platoon cohesion by focusing Soldiers on success and actively combating sexual harassment and assault and equal opportunity issues. To be effective, standards need to be properly enforced through counseling, corrective training, and the Uniform Code of Military Justice (UCMJ).

High standards focus a platoon on success and create goals for individuals and teams to achieve. This helps build a team by creating a sense of ownership and pride in the platoon.

PLs and PSGs must always be on the lookout for issues regarding hazing and sexual assault. Hazing and sexual assault destroy trust and the cohesion of teams. Leaders who create and enforce a zero-tolerance policy on hazing supporting their commander's policies can help create a positive atmosphere in their platoon. Care must be taken when building rite-of-passage programs into the platoon to ensure they do not cross into hazing.

Well-disciplined platoons follow Army standards and brigade, battalion, and company policy letters. New leaders should read and understand their unit's policy letters and make their subordinates do the same. When a Soldier is arrested for driving under the influence, who needs to know? What happens when a positive drug test is returned? What about an underage drinking issue in barracks? Leaders who do not know the standards cannot enforce them.

For Platoon Leaders

Be involved in all levels of reward, corrective actions, and punishment at the platoon level. Punishment is reserved for the commander through the UCMJ process. Be very careful of punishment disguised as corrective training; this can lead to indiscipline in the platoon. Successful PSGs and squad leaders keep the PL informed of all corrective actions and rewards. If junior leaders are found punishing Soldiers outside of their authority, it must be stopped. Listen to your NCOs; they have more interaction with the Soldier in question and knowledge of the situation. Working together and keeping company leadership informed will prevent issues with hazing and harassment.

"*PLs should be kept apprised of everything that is going on within their platoon. Granted, they can let the NCOs handle the smaller discipline issues, but the PL still needs to know there are discipline issues and what those issues are.*"

— Former PL[4]

Platoon-level leaders have multiple tools at their hands to enforce discipline in their platoon. PLs and PSGs can counsel, give corrective training, and recommend UCMJ to the commander.

Counseling is often the first step and should be in writing and include a detailed plan of action for the Soldier to improve performance. Counseling is a two-way conversation, even for negative performance. Most times, a Soldier will hint at family or personal issues affecting their work. Listen and get Soldiers the help they need as discussed in the family readiness section. Proactive counseling can stop small issues before they become major and require more drastic measures. Assessing and counseling a close coworker (squad leader or PSG) on his deficiencies can be difficult. A leader owes it to their Soldiers and NCOs to give them honest feedback to help them improve. PLs and PSGs also owe it to the Army to write honest and accurate assessments of their subordinates to ensure the right people are promoted to higher levels of leadership.

Corrective actions and training are effective tools to fix training deficiencies, either on the spot or over time. Stopping a Soldier backing up a vehicle without a ground guide and providing an immediate demonstration on how to safely back up a vehicle with a ground guide is an example of an on-the-spot corrective action. Providing extra preliminary markmanship instruction (PMI) to Soldiers unable to qualify on their assigned weapon is an example of applying corrective training over time. Care must be taken to ensure corrective actions and training are not oppressive, do not single out Soldiers, directly relate to the training deficiency, and do not continue after the deficiency is overcome. Documenting corrective actions and training on a counseling statement and keeping the company command team informed can help prevent training from becoming hazing or harassment.

The following definitions are from U.S. Army Training and Doctrine Command (TRADOC) Regulation 350-6, Enlisted Initial Entry Training Policies and Administration:[5]

> **Corrective Action**. Nonpunitive actions used as a motivational tool by authorized NCOs to immediately address deficiencies in performance or conduct and to reinforce required standards. By virtue of administering corrective action, there is recognition that the misconduct did not result from intentional or gross failure to comply with standards of military conduct. Corrective action is inappropriate for situations requiring additional training to master a specific level of skill proficiency, or in matters where punishment is administered as a result of UCMJ action.
>
> **Corrective Training**. Corrective training is for Soldiers who have demonstrated that they need, and would benefit from, additional instruction or practice in a particular skill. Corrective training should be directly related to the military skill that the Soldier is deficient in and assist him in meeting the standard.

A last step for most Soldier issues is recommending UCMJ to the commander. The company commander can execute bars to reenlistment, chapters for separation, summary Article 15s, and company-grade Article 15s. Company commanders can only recommend field-grade Article 15s and court martial to the battalion commander. Work closely with company leadership to assemble counseling statements and other statements needed to document the event. Commanders work their discipline programs differently. Open and honest communication helps platoon-level leaders understand how to support their commander's program.

For Platoon Sergeants

You have seen and perhaps been on the receiving end of negative counseling, corrective training, and UCMJ. Your PL has not. Help him through this process. It is often difficult for a young leader to work through. Also, work in close conjunction with the 1SG. Your 1SG has a direct line to the commander and can help review counseling, develop corrective training programs, and decide whether to recommend UCMJ or not.

Family Readiness Programs

"Ten percent of my Soldiers take up 90 percent of my time. Dealing with family issues and taking care of Soldiers is just what PSGs do. When I am in a company with a solid family readiness program, I know I can focus on training when we are in the field because there is someone there that families can go to first before trying to contact their Soldier."

— Infantry PSG

Supporting a company's family readiness group (FRG) program and Soldier's families is a critical part of maintaining readiness within a platoon. PLs and PSGs are integral parts of a company's FRG or program. The FRG is the commander's forum for communicating to the families of Soldiers. It is a spouse's direct link to company leadership. As senior leaders within the company, platoon-level leaders should encourage their platoon's participation, plan and attend meetings, and be part of their Soldier's family link with the company.

There are several ways to support the company's FRG and encourage participation. Adjusting schedules and finding time for Soldiers and their families to attend meetings can help accomplish this. When planning training at the platoon level, leaders need to be aware of how events affect families and the company FRG.

Platoon-level leaders are often selected to plan and attend FRG meetings. While seen as an additional duty, FRG meetings should be briefed and tracked in the company training meeting as part of the training calendar. Oftentimes, the action officer works with the company FRG leader to plan and prepare the meeting. The FRG leader brings a wealth of knowledge and insight, but the action officer is responsible for detailed planning based on the troop-leading procedures (TLPs). Some commanders make use of social media using company newsletters, Facebook Live chat, and other means of talking directly to families.

Dealing with Soldiers' families can be a challenging process. Being proactive and identifying possible issues through engagement with Soldiers and the FRG helps identify high-risk Soldiers. A first line of defense is the battalion chaplain. The chaplain has access to programs and training to help Soldiers through difficult times.

Army Community Services (ACS) is another excellent resource for a platoon. ACS provides multiple programs such as Army Emergency Relief loans, relocation assistance, employment readiness for spouses, financial training, budgeting classes, and other programs. ACS also has the ability to refer Soldiers and families to other Army resources. It is often a critical first step for leaders to refer Soldiers who need assistance. Army One Source, online at www.myarmyonesource.com, is another ACS-type resource that can link Soldiers and families into the Army's support structure. A final resource is a unit's military family life counselor.

Endnotes

1. DA Form 5988-E, *Equipment Maintenance and Inspection Worksheet (EGA)*, 01 MAR 1991. See https://armypubs.army.mil.

2. GCSS-A Smartbook, page 22. Available online at https://gcss.army.mil/Documents/Training/GCSS-Army%20Smart%20Book%20-%20Plant%20Maintenance%20v7.pdf.

3. Ibid., page 23.

4. LT Brock Young. "What NOT to do as a Platoon Leader," in *Company Command*, December 2013, page 53. Available online at https://www.usma.edu/caldol/siteassets/armymagazine/docs/2013/CC_ARMY_(Dec2013)_What_NOT_to_do.pdf.

5. TRADOC Regulation 350-6, *Enlisted Initial Entry Training Policies and Administration*, 20 MAR 2017, page 87.

Chapter 4
Execution

Overview

Unfortunately, a platoon leader (PL) and platoon sergeant's (PSG's) time in a platoon is limited. A leader's time in a platoon often culminates during a situational training exercise, live-fire exercise (LFX), a combat training center (CTC) rotation, or deployment. The PL and PSG must understand in detail how to receive a mission, prepare a mission brief, and execute that mission with their platoon. There are many missions platoons are asked to do, but they all have some basic requirements in common that make them successful.

This chapter discusses troop-leading procedures (TLPs), patrolling, integrating enablers, and after action reviews (AARs).

Troop-Leading Procedures

> "*Being a PL is not like in the movies. No one hangs off your every word and you cannot do it all yourself. Your PSG is right 90 percent of the time and you need to use your whole team to plan, rehearse, and execute if you want to be successful.*"
>
> — PL on his return from Iraq

Platoon-level leaders plan and issue orders using TLPs. TLPs help focus leaders' thoughts and ensure they execute planning to standard. Planning using TLPs must be timely, collaborative, detailed, and properly briefed to subordinates to prepare a platoon for its mission.

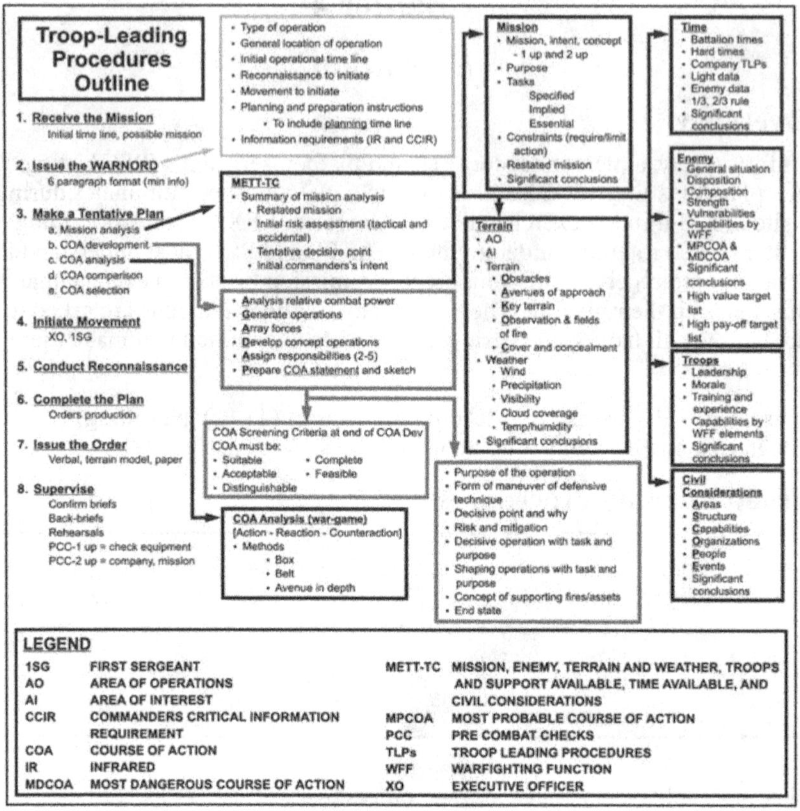

Figure 4-1. Troop-leading procedures outline[1]

An understanding of time is important during TLP planning. During step 1. Receive the Mission; and step 7. Issue the Order, PLs and PSGs should be thinking about "who needs to know." Providing the initial warning order (WARNORD) in a timely manner and to the right Soldiers allows junior leaders to start planning for the mission (for example, letting a squad leader know his squad will provide a support by fire allows him to task-organize and prepare the squad, or letting attached engineers know the composition of an obstacle will allow them to have the right equipment to breach). As a rule of thumb, leaders use the one-third, two-thirds rule. A senior leader should issue an order using one third of the available planning time, giving junior leaders two thirds of the available time for planning and rehearsals. This is difficult, but using preformatted operation orders (OPORDs) enables leaders to identify information shortfalls in the plan and to rapidly and efficiently develop the platoon OPORD.

Applying "who needs to know" to planning extends past issuing orders to include collaborative planning. Here, a PSG is a critical part of the process. PLs are usually taught to focus on the mission and actions on the objective. They often leave logistical and medical concerns for the PSGs. This division of labor may lead to quicker planning, but PSGs often have the experience necessary to refine actions on the objective to help the platoon accomplish its mission. Planning using TLPs is a collaborative event that uses the strengths of the PL, PSG, squad leaders, technical experts within the platoon, and any attached enablers.

For Platoon Leaders

PLs lead and are responsible for the platoon's planning process. This can create a stressful situation where PLs feel they must accomplish everything alone. This is untrue and is a point of failure for many inexperienced PLs.

After assuming a leadership position, sit down with your PSG and squad leaders and decide how your platoon will plan. Setting expectations and building standard operating procedures (SOPs) now will prepare your platoon for success while deployed or at a LFX or CTC. That said, not all PSGs are created equal. You have a company executive officer (XO) and first sergeant (1SG) for mentorship while you build your team and prepare your platoon.

For Platoon Sergeants

You are the most experienced member of your platoon. Your knowledge is needed in all aspects of planning to refine your PL's plan. That said, not all PLs are created equal. Provide input during steps one through six of the TLPs. When your PL issues his order, realize that any disagreements during planning need to be forgotten during supervision and your platoon's execution. Your squad leaders will look up to you. Any disagreement or resentment between you and your platoon leader will create an atmosphere that will destroy your platoon's cohesion.

Effective TLPs use detailed planning that focus on mission, enemy, terrain and weather, troops and support available, time available, and civilian considerations (METT-TC). Many PLs take the easy path and do not conduct their own mission analysis or develop graphic control measures. They instead rely on the company order. For example, movement to the objective is often overlooked or glossed over. Movement on foot over uneven terrain can be as slow as 1 kilometer per hour. Mounted movement is faster, but leaders must plan for mounting, dismounting, and gaining accountability. Overlooking a small detail like movement can de-synchronize an entire operation. There are multiple ways to integrate mission analysis, course of action development, and analysis during planning.

Detailed rehearsals (minimum movement, actions on contact, actions on the objective, and consolidation/reorganization) are part of TLPs. Leaders use rehearsals to confirm their plan, identify any friction points, and see their platoon in time and space. Rehearsals can also be a supplement to an OPORD brief. In addition to rehearsals, PSGs and squad leaders should host precombat checks (PCCs) and precombat inspections (PCIs).

PLs should resist the urge to abbreviate their OPORDs and ensure they give junior leaders a full brief on the patrol. If possible, all enablers and members of the platoon should attend. Brief thoroughly, using terrain models, concept sketches, and other visual and verbal mediums. Allow junior leaders to brief their relevant portions. This allows them to take ownership and demonstrate mastery of their mission tasks. Everyone in the platoon needs to understand the mission. A best practice is to summarize a tactical OPORD with an intent: "we are going here and then we will defeat the enemy" or "we are getting Class IV from here to there, so Alpha Company can emplace obstacles." This gives the platoon a single focus and empowers junior leaders to be flexible while getting the mission done. After issuing the order, the PL runs a backbrief to ensure the platoon understands the mission from start to finish.

Timely, collaborative, detailed, and properly briefed plans are important as a platoon. Leaders often focus on actions on the objective, but planning, rehearsing, and conducting PCCs and PCIs prepare a platoon for its mission and sets platoon leadership up to accomplish the mission.

Patrolling

> *1. Don't forget nothing.*
>
> *2. Have your musket clean as a whistle, hatchet scoured, sixty rounds powder and ball, and be ready to march at a minute's warning.*
>
> *3. When we march, we keep moving till dark, so as to give the enemy the least possible chance at us.*
>
> *4. When we camp, half the party stays awake while the other half sleeps.*
>
> *5. Don't ever march home the same way. Take a different route so you won't be ambushed.*
>
> *6. No matter whether we travel in big parties or little ones, each party has to keep a scout 20 yards ahead, 20 yards on each flank, and 20 yards in the rear, so the main body can't be surprised and wiped out.*
>
> *7. Don't sleep beyond dawn. Dawn's when the French and Indians attack.*
>
> — Revised from Major Robert Rangers' "28 Rules of Ranging" c. 1789[2]

Platoons execute a multitude of tasks based on the type of platoon, current operation, and other requirements. Most tasks can be classified as a patrol of some type: a detachment sent out by a larger unit to conduct a specific mission that operates semi-independently and returns to the main body upon completion of the mission.[3] This methodology works for almost all missions, whether it is a tactical patrol or a funeral detail. PLs and PSGs need a baseline knowledge of patrolling and the ability to organize their platoon and lead a patrol. Typically, the PL will operate as the patrol leader and the PSG operates as the assistant patrol leader. When planning and executing each patrol, PLs and PSGs use the principles of patrolling: planning, reconnaissance, security, control, and common sense.

For Platoon Leaders

As a PL, you are typically the patrol leader when operating as a platoon. As the patrol leader, you are expected to:

- Lead planning in accordance with the TLPs.
- Lead rehearsals.
- Ensure the patrol maintains security at all times.
- Place yourself where you are most needed to accomplish the mission.
- Execute a leader's reconnaissance to confirm your plan.
- Maneuver squads and integrate and coordinate organic and nonorganic weapon systems in contact.
- Provide accurate and timely reporting on your patrol's status.

For Platoon Sergeants

As a PSG, you are typically the assistant patrol leader when operating as a platoon. As the assistant patrol leader you are expected to:

- Be prepared to assume the patrol leader role if needed.
- Assist the patrol leader as needed.
- Uphold standards and discipline.
- Maintain accountability of equipment and people.
- Establish the casualty collection point and coordinate and execute casualty evacuation.
- Manage the unit's combat load and monitor the patrol's logistical status.

Patrols are planned missions. Even a simple movement between forward operating bases requires detailed planning and rehearsals. Platoon-level leaders use TLPs to plan their mission starting with actions on the objective, backward to departure from friendly lines, forward to reentry to friendly lines,[4] and actions on contact. The OPORD is briefed using the five-paragraph format to the platoon and any attachments and then reinforced with rehearsals. In some situations, the time available for planning may be minimal. Having an effective platoon tactical standard operating procedure (TACSOP); rehearsed battle drills; applying the one-third, two-thirds rule; and using collaborative and parallel planning help a platoon plan quickly.

Reconnaissance is a critical part of any mission. Reconnaissance starts during the planning phase with map and route reconnaissance. Patrol leaders also should coordinate with the S-2 to determine the current threat composition and disposition while planning. During the mission, reconnaissance is used to confirm the threat composition and disposition. For example, a patrol leader leading a logistics patrol uses map and route reconnaissance along with information from the S-2 to determine likely improvised explosive device and ambush locations. During the mission, the leader changes the patrol's movement technique and formation as needed. This allows the forward element to make visual contact or contact with the smallest possible element with the enemy before being decisively engaged. When at the objective, it is critical for the PL to make a leader's reconnaissance, allowing him to confirm the plan.

The principle of security allows a platoon to conserve combat power until it is needed on the objective. Platoon-level patrols usually provide security internally, but may work in conjunction with other platoons such as a combined arms route clearance operation. Patrol leaders and assistant patrol leaders who foster an aggressive posture can deter enemy action and identify and react quickly when needed. Ensuring Soldiers are actively scanning their sectors, adjusting movement techniques and formation based on the threat, and encouraging crosstalk to pass off targets all help maintain an aggressive security posture. Planning and rehearsing security operations occurs during TLPs by identifying rally points, en route target reference points, and rehearsing actions on contact.

> *"While conducting offensive operations, rotational units have difficulty with maintaining proper security during patrol base activities, short halts, and at rally points. After the first 24 hours of the joint forcible entry as units become tired, their security posture can drop significantly. Over the course of the rotation, many units struggle to enforce security and the priorities of work. For example, Soldiers execute "rucksack flops," pull security from their backs, fail to find cover, and fail to maintain their weapons at all times.*
>
> *Soldiers cannot be allowed to let their discomfort supersede the main principle of patrolling. Units fail to train endurance and fail to enforce the standards over a long period of time. The drop in security can start with a failure of individual Soldier discipline once Soldiers become tired, hot, and hungry. Security continues to fail because leaders, especially team leaders, do not troop the line to make Soldiers pull security properly."*
>
> — Observation by an observer controller at the Joint Readiness Training Center[5]

Whether a patrol is a combat patrol (raid, ambush, or security patrol), reconnaissance patrol, or escorting fuelers between two locations, once a patrol makes contact with an enemy force, the patrol's mission is to destroy or neutralize the enemy in order to allow the patrol to complete its original mission. As actions on contact are briefed in the order and rehearsed, squad and team leaders should know how to react, either to fight through or to neutralize and continue the mission. As soon as possible, a spot report using the size, activity, location, unit, time, and equipment (SALUTE) format should be given to higher along with the patrol's actions. This report is critical to facilitate support from higher headquarters and to inform follow-on units of the enemy threat. During contact, patrol leaders integrate and coordinate outside elements such as indirect fires, and control internal elements such as rates of fire (cyclic, rapid, and sustained) and maneuver. Assistant patrol leaders assist the patrol leader and prepare to execute casualty evacuation as needed. Following contact, once the enemy has been destroyed or the unit has reached a safe location, patrol leaders receive ammunition, casualty, and equipment (ACE) reports to assess their unit and then consolidate them as needed to complete the patrol.

Patrol leaders and assistant patrol leaders control their platoons throughout patrolling operations. Before the mission, outlining standardized reports, check points, phase lines, and other control measures allows leaders to gain an understanding of the battlefield and the patrols status. Doing this also gives leeway to adjust a mission during execution. In addition to planning, leaders control their platoon through PCCs, PCIs, and backbriefs while supervising their platoon. Successful control does not require centralized decision making at the platoon level. Successful control provides a framework to squad leaders, empowering them to execute the mission within the commander's intent.

PLs and PSGs must apply common sense. If something does not feel right, it probably is not. PLs and PSGs must trust their instincts and learn to use each other as sounding boards. Each leader brings different knowledge and experiences, and in working together, PLs and PSGs check each other.

Patrolling is a fundamental mission of the platoon. Despite differences among types of platoons and functions, look at each mission as a patrol. Whether the patrol is a movement between two locations, a raid, or a funeral detail, leaders use the principles of patrolling (planning, reconnaissance, security, control, and common sense) to ensure success. Additional information on patrolling can be found in Chapter 6 of ATP 3-21.8.

Integrating Enablers

> *"I can tell you if a platoon will be successful or not during the first hour. Those PLs and PSGs who don't engage us, listen to our advice, and make us part of their platoon fail. Those that let us brief during the order, integrate us into their movement and planning are able to get us where we need to be, when we need to be, to open a lane through the obstacle and get the platoon onto the objective."*
>
> — A Sapper team leader briefing his company commander

Enablers are a key part of any combined arms mission. PLs and PSGs who plan for, integrate, and empower enablers turn them into force multipliers. Those who do not, risk being unable to mass effects at the decisive point of the battle.

Today's battlefield often requires attachments and enablers down to the platoon level. These technical experts can either be fully integrated in a patrol such as Sappers moving with the platoon and executing a breach on the objective, or merely provide support when needed such as an attack weapons team (AWT) of helicopters providing direct fire support during an engagement. Whether attached or supporting, leaders should plan with and for enablers. For example, the Sappers in the above example should be involved in the platoon plan and brief actions at the breach, along with the marking system for the lane. Platoon leaders should plan for high-value and high-payoff targets along with a task and purpose for the AWT above. Therefore, if needed, they can be quickly focused on where they can provide the best support.

An indirect-fire support plan is a critical part of a patrol's plan and needs to be planned and integrated the same as other enablers. Fires should be planned at a minimum along the route to the objective, on any suspected enemy positions, on the objective, and beyond the objective to enable maneuver. Having en route target reference points allows a leader to adjust fire off a known point if needed. Leaders also need to know the location of fire support and their ranges to understand the support they can receive. When planning a raid or other combat patrol, leaders should carefully plan the echelonment of fires, turning on and off fire support as a platoon approaches an objective to maintain constant fire on the enemy (discussed in detail in ATP 3-21.8, Appendix C). Some platoons will have a forward observer (FO) to assist during planning and execution. However, without an FO, the platoon leader needs to plan for and be prepared to call for fires.

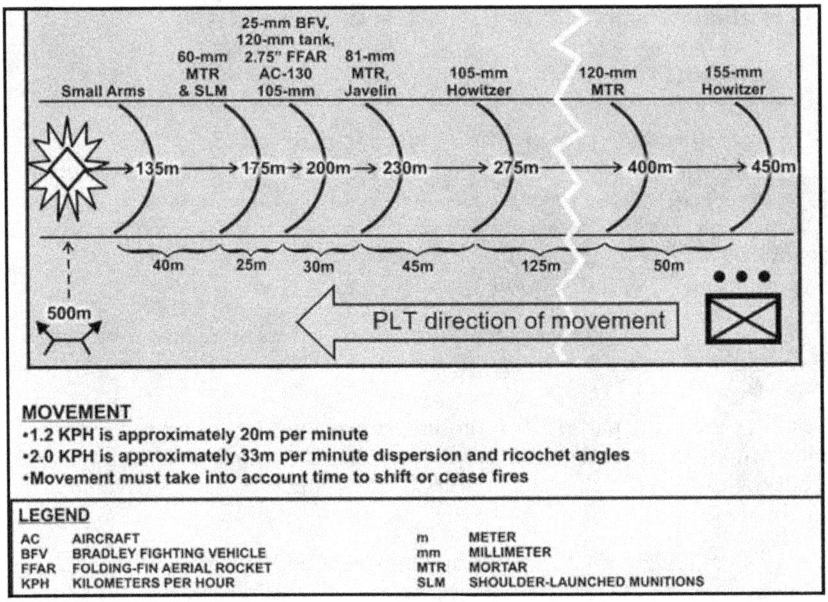

Figure 4-2. Offensive echelonment of fires[6]

For Platoon Leaders

As the lead planner for your platoon, it is important to understand the capabilities and limitations of your enablers in order to employ them at the decisive point. When a supporting element arrives, your first question should be "what do you bring to the fight?" The second question should be "what support do you need from my platoon?" After receiving answers, make sure the supporting element is included during planning and participates in the rehearsals.

Sometimes, due to short timelines, an enabler may not link-up with the platoon until at the line of departure. Provide a quick fragmentary order with task and purpose at a minimum. If possible, plan training events at home station with enablers you may work with at a CTC or during deployment to build interoperability and habitual relationships. SOPs can be built into TACSOPs to streamline this process. Finally, take care of any attached enablers just as well as you do your platoon. This fosters trust and confidence in your leadership.

Integrate enablers and attachments into the platoon as soon as they arrive. The company TACSOP should have an SOP for attachments and detachments that ensures a task and purpose is provided, radios and call signs are communicated, and food and billets are planned for. In addition to receiving the elements, they should be included in planning and patrol briefs to ensure they are properly employed at the decisive point.

For Platoon Sergeants

As your PL welcomes attachments and starts planning with them, be sure to link them into your platoon support functions. Their numbers should be added for chow, housing, fuel, and other support functions. Your master authorization list, personnel status report, and patrol trip tickets may also need to be updated with the appropriate information. In addition, an attachment may have special needs (for example, an increased fuel consumption or demolitions and other special ammunition). You and your PL may use the example enabler checklist (see Figure 4-3) to codify a process to receive and integrate enablers into your platoon.

Enabler Checklist

Date Time Group (DTG): ________________________
Enabler: Unit__________________
Officer in Charge (OIC)_________________________
Noncommissioned Officer in Charge (NCOIC)_______
Gaining Unit: Unit__________
OIC_______________
NCOIC____________

Provided From Enabler:

By vehicle: Standard name lines, battle roster number, allergies, blood type, sensitive items by serial number, other special equipment

By position: Call signs, location, order of march

Statuses: Classes I, II, and V; any equipment deadlines or restrictions

Special Capabilities: Mission capabilities

Provided to Enabler:

Expectations

OPORD: Task and purpose, rehearsals, etc.

Communications: Call signs; frequencies; Primary, Alternate, Contingency, and Emergency (PACE) plan

Figure 4-3. Enabler checklist

Most leaders are experts in their craft but may have limited knowledge in the capabilities and restrictions of attached units. A way to bridge this knowledge gap and empower attached elements is to have them provide a capabilities brief to the widest possible audience. This gives attachments the chance to demonstrate their proficiency and allows squad and team leaders the chance to understand how to employ them. Attachments should also be included in rehearsals for movement, actions on contact, actions on the objective, consolidation/reorganization, and other key actions during the operation.

Trends at the CTCs show that most attachments rarely attend OPORDs and never brief during OPORDs, even if it is just to explain their capabilities and restrictions.[7] With the operational tempo and the way the Army task-organizes for combined arms operations, platoon-level leaders need to plan for, integrate, and empower enablers. PLs and PSGs who do not, risk being unable to employ and synchronize assets at the decisive point.

After Action Reviews

> *"I have my platoon do an AAR after each training event. The largest pitfall leaders have is talking about something that was going to happen anyway. Leaders need to focus on what they can control within their scope to improve the organization. We should not focus on what we cannot control."*
>
> — Infantry PSG

AARs are an opportunity for a leader to facilitate learning from training events or operations and to improve future performance. At the platoon level, AARs are used to assess team, squad, and platoon performance and to provide feedback to company leadership. Leaders should understand the difference between formal and informal AARs, how to plan and facilitate a review, and what to do with the results of their AARs.

Platoon-level leaders use both formal and informal AARs to encourage their platoons to learn and improve. A formal AAR is a planned event that is led by an external facilitator. Usually, formal AARs follow training events and they provide an environment for platoons to assess their performance and identify ways to improve. Informal AARs are used to improve performance during training and often take the form of on-the-spot coaching. PLs and PSGs are the lead trainers of their platoon and correct Soldiers as necessary during training.

Leaders use the plan, prepare, execute, and assess model for AARs. Using this model, AARs should be planned into and after training. At a minimum, leaders should plan for a facilitator, location, and time for each AAR. When executing lane training or repetitive training, an AAR should be planned after each iteration to identify what should be sustained or improved for the next lane, allowing for learning and improvement. Preparing for an AAR takes place before the training event by collecting appropriate training and evaluation outlines (T&EOs) and during the training event by collecting observations for further discussion.

Both formal and informal AARs are executed similarly. The facilitator should start with summarizing the event, move into identifying what should be sustained and what should be improved, and finally determining how to execute differently. See Figure 4-4 for an AAR script. Facilitators should ensure maximum participation of the unit, opposing force, and observer–coach/trainers, etc. If possible, arrange to have the discussion on the same training site. Multiple viewpoints help units see blind spots they may miss.

AAR Script

What was supposed to happen, what was the plan?

What actually happened?

Why did this occur?

What did we learn from this?

What should we change for future operations?

What training do we need to conduct to improve?

Figure 4-4. AAR script

After the AAR, platoon-level leaders should analyze and learn from the results. Units that hand-wave the AAR process and get "three ups" and "three downs" and then move on, miss a golden opportunity. Leaders should assess their platoon using the plan, prepare, execute, and assess model and retrain or revise SOPs. In addition to internal learning, the platoon's lessons and best practices should be shared with the company and other PLs and PSGs. Finally, any action plans should be included in counseling to ensure the platoon continues to learn and improve.

AARs are covered in detail in Field Manual 7-0, *Train to Win in a Complex World* (05 OCT 2016), Appendix D. Platoon-level leaders should review the appendix when planning training events. At a minimum, PLs and PSGs should know the differences of formal and informal AARs, how to plan and facilitate a review, and learn from the results of their AARs.

Endnotes

1. ATP 3-21.8, *Infantry Platoon and Squad,* 12 APR 2016, page A-4.

2. "75th Ranger Regiment: Robert Rogers' Standing Orders" on U.S. Army Web Page at https://www.goarmy.com/ranger/about-the-rangers/rodgers-orders.html.

3. ATP 3-21.8, page 6-1.

4. Ibid., page 6-3.

5. Joint Readiness Training Center Operations Group, Center for Army Lessons Learned, *News from the CTC: Attack! Insights and Issues with the Brigade Combat Team Offense in a Decisive Action Training Environment (DATE)*, 23 JAN 2018. (Authorized users only, CAC login required)

6. Revised from Figure C-1 in ATP 3-21.8, page C-5.

Chapter 5
Vignettes

Overview

Leaders at all levels learn best through the experience of others. There have been many platoon leaders (PLs) and platoon sergeants (PSGs) who can share their experiences with future PLs and PSGs. Leaders can also do well through a professional reading program aimed at expanding a leader's knowledge, which can introduce them to new situations and develop critical thinking skills.

This chapter consists of four vignettes that provide insights into the experiences of Army leaders. These can be used as a discussion with a partner PL or PSG on how each would react. This exercise can build leadership skills as a team and prepare a platoon for success.

Vignette 1

It has been three months since Second Lieutenant (2LT) Adams was assigned as a PL. His PSG, Sergeant First Class (SFC) Sharp, has been the PSG for the past year since the company's last deployment. Their brigade is deploying to the National Training Center (NTC) and just completed packing and sealing containers. Because it is the end of the month, 2LT Adams knows he has to sign his hand receipt as part of the company battle rhythm.

When reviewing his hand receipt and packing lists (Department of Army [DA] Form 1750, Packing List), 2LT Adams could not find one of the platoon's weapon mounts annotated. 2LT Adams knows he told SFC Sharp that the company commander wanted the platoon to bring all of their weapon mounts. Because the platoon was training last week, they were unable to pack and seal containers until Tuesday. 2LT Adams and SFC Sharp were preparing for the company training meeting and had Staff Sergeant (SSG) Engel pack and seal the platoon's container.

2LT Adams searched the platoon's equipment locker and did not find the mount. SSG Engel said he was sure the weapon mount was packed. SFC Sharp knows the platoon had property issues with the last platoon leader and the turnover to 2LT Adams could have been better. With the time crunch, 2LT Adams had not completed his sub hand receipts.

The company supply sergeant knocks on the platoon office door and shares, "The executive officer (XO) wanted me to give you a copy of your hand receipt. The commander said no one goes home until he gets signed hand receipts from each platoon."

- How should 2LT Adams and SFC Sharp address the issue?
- How could 2LT Adams and SFC Sharp have prevented this situation from occurring?
- When and how should 2LT Adams and SFC Sharp address the issue with company leadership?
- What controls can 2LT Adams and SFC Sharp implement to prevent this from happening again?

Vignette 2

While at NTC, 2LT Adams and SFC Sharp's platoon moves to the support by fire for the company breach. 2LT Adams is following the platoon's movement on his Joint Capabilities Release (JCR) when he notices that his Global Positioning System (GPS) is no longer updating his location. He contacts SFC Sharp who reports the same effect on his GPS. 2LT Adams attempts to contact his company commander, but is unable to raise him on communications.

SSG Engel, the lead squad leader, reports that he thinks he reached the support-by-fire location, but cannot confirm due to his GPS not working. 2LT Adams is unsure if he is in the right location. Although he has a map and compass, he is unable to find himself on it due to the darkness and lack of identifiable terrain.

SFC Sharp reports that he and the third squad leader think they can identify the obstacle and an enemy overwatch position past it with their night vision goggles. SFC Sharp wants to set the support by fire in this location.

2LT Adams knows that if they are in the wrong position, they may de-synchronize the rest of the company. The platoon may be in the right spot, but what if his platoon went too far? He tries to check his GPS and contact the company again, but has no luck.

As 2LT Adams looks at his watch, he realizes he is supposed to start the suppression in five minutes. Over the radio, SFC Sharp starts telling the squad leaders to set the support by fire here.

- What should 2LT Adams and SFC Sharp do?
- How should 2LT Adams and SFC Sharp resolve their differences of opinion while on mission?

- How could 2LT Adams and SFC Sharp have either prevented this situation during planning or mitigated it when it occurred?
- Would a common set of graphic control measures help?
- How would you expect a squad leader to act if the above scenario was about a squad setting a support by fire for a platoon breach?

Vignette 3

After a successful NTC rotation, 2LT Adams and SFC Sharp's platoon returned to home station. During their first company training meeting, CPT Sherman said the company was going to start a training path that will culminate in six months when the brigade certifies companies with a combined arms live-fire exercise (CALFEX). CPT Sherman stressed the company needs to be able to shoot (shoot expert on their assigned weapon systems), move (day and night driver's training and mounted movement techniques), and communicate (radio and JCR training, including operating in a GPS- and communications-degraded situation). First Sergeant (1SG) Willis reviewed the company's statistics; the platoons were behind on the noncommissioned officer evaluation reports (NCOERs), and Medical Protection System (MEDPROS) showed most Soldiers amber or red on something.

After the training meeting, 2LT Adams and SFC Sharp sat down in their platoon office. 2LT Adams pulled up the company training calendar showing the required 350-1 training and service schedule for their vehicles. SFC Sharp looked at his Army physical fitness test tracker and reviewed the MEDPROS tracker.

2LT Adams stated that he thought the squads needed to get out in the field and start working on battle drills for team and squad live fires needed for the company CALFEX. SFC Sharp looked at his numbers and recommended they start with physical training and focus the squad leaders on medical appointments.

As they start reviewing the Army Training Network (ATN) website and laying out their platoon's training for the next couple months, the operations sergeant walks in. "SFC Sharp, a new tasking from battalion just came in. They need a platoon to assist on gate guard next month and the 1SG told me to give it to you."

- How do 2LT Adams and SFC Sharp decide what and how to train to prepare their platoon?
- How can their platoon best manage the multitude of requirements that are put on it and maintain readiness?

- What can 2LT Adams and SFC Sharp do to keep platoon cohesion and discipline given their operational tempo?

Vignette 4

1LT Adams and SFC Sharp returned from their company's squad live-fire exercise. SSG Engel did well, as expected, but Third Squad had some retraining to do. SFC Sharp predicted this, Sergeant (SGT) Young, Third Squad's Alpha Team leader, did not participate. He had another Army Substance Abuse Program (ASAP) class.

SGT Young was the best tactical team leader when the platoon was at NTC, but he was starting to be unreliable. Last week, he missed physical training in the morning claiming his alarm did not go off.

At the family readiness group (FRG) meeting before NTC, SGT Young and his wife got into a fight. It appeared that SGT Young's wife was frustrated about the NTC rotation and was taking it out on the team leader. SGT Young brushed it off. At NTC, SGT Young was critical, being able to complete a resection, figuring out where the platoon was as they set in a support by fire.

After returning from NTC and being relieved off gate duty, the platoon went into overdrive, preparing for the company CALFEX, often staying until 1800 or 1900 hours. SGT Young's team worked well together, but there were rumors they would go out drinking together after work. SGT Young's wife also did not attend the last FRG meeting.

A couple weeks ago, SGT Young and his team were reported by the charge of quarters (CQ) for partying in a Soldier's barracks room. The commander referred the whole team to ASAP because there was alcohol involved. Still, the following Monday, SGT Young took his team to the range and they all qualified expert.

As 1LT Adams and SFC Sharp pulled into the company, the XO was waiting for them. SGT Young was arrested last night for driving under the influence and the company commander wanted 1LT Adams and SFC Sharp to report to his office immediately.

- How should 1LT Adams and SFC Sharp address the issue?
- How could 1LT Adams and SFC Sharp have either prevented this situation or mitigated it as it occurred?
- How does the platoon maintain its cohesion and discipline?
- What resources are available for SGT Young and his wife?

Appendix A
Platoon Smartbook

Overview

Throughout their time in leadership, platoon leaders (PLs) and platoon sergeants (PSGs) should maintain a leader smartbook. This leader smartbook provides the PL and PSG easy access to platoon-specific information they need. When combined with the property book and company and battalion tactical standard operating procedures (TACSOPs), platoon-level leaders will have what they need to accomplish their missions.

Recommended smartbook items:

- Personnel roster (include home addresses and contact information)
- Platoon battle roster
- Platoon training tracker (see Figure A-1) (Army physical fitness training [APFT], weapons qualification, drivers training, crew certification, etc.)
- Vehicle tracker (include subsystems and associated weapons)
- Maintenance tracker
- Master authorization list (MAL)
- Training schedule (eight weeks out)
- Preformatted operation order (OPORD) (to receive the mission and facilitate planning)
- Preformatted reports (medical evacuation [MEDEVAC], spot, unexploded ordnance [UXO], etc.)
- Company commander's and battalion commander's priorities and intent
- Platoon property book
- Company TACSOP
- Battalion TACSOP

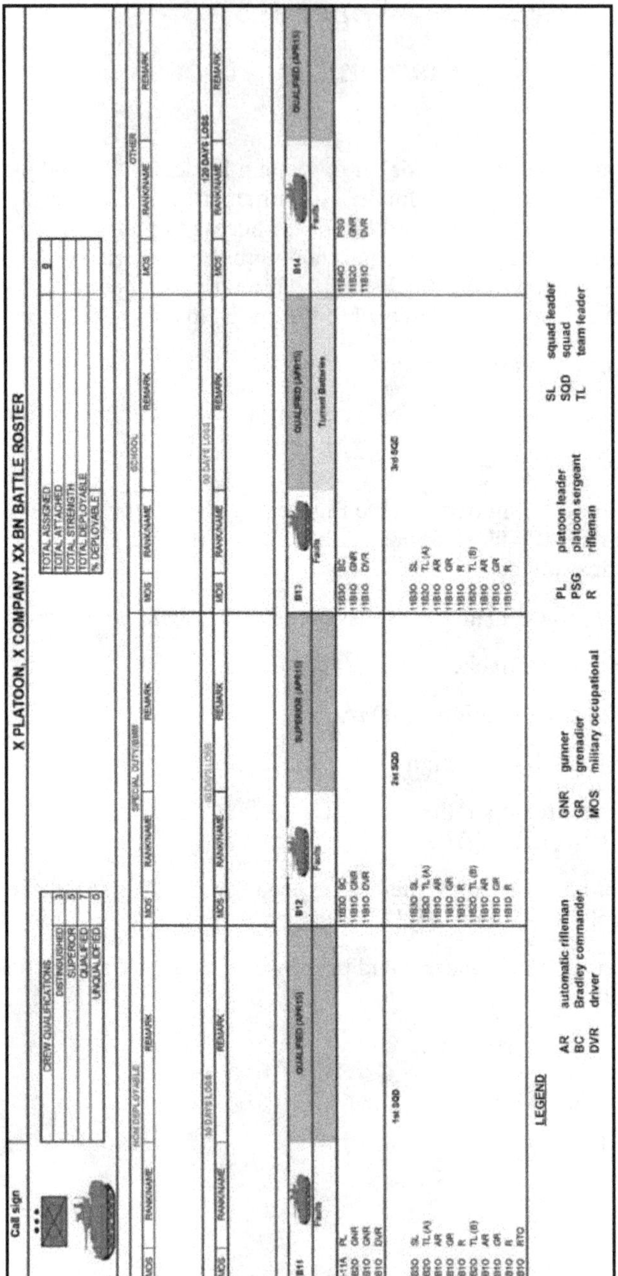

Figure A-1. Battle roster

Appendix B

Platoon Resource Library

Overview

Platoons should compile a library of relevant information to facilitate learning and accomplishment of their mission. This resource library can be digital; however, platoons can benefit from hard copies when available for use at the range and during opportunity training.

Graphic training aids (GTAs). GTAs can be picked up or ordered at an installation training support center (TSC). GTAs produced by the Center for Army Lessons Learned (CALL) can be downloaded and printed from the CALL restricted website at https://call2.army.mil/Login.aspx (authorized users only, CAC login required).

Technical manuals (TMs). TMs can be downloaded and printed from the Electronic Technical Manual (ETM) application on the U.S. Army Materiel Command Logistics Support Activity (LOGSA) website at https://liw.logsa.army.mil (authorized users only, CAC login required) or see the company publications clerk.

Field manuals (FMs); Army doctrine publications (ADPs); Army doctrine reference publications (ADRPs); Army techniques publications (ATPs); Army tactics, techniques, and procedures (ATTPs); and training circulars (TCs). Download and print from the Army Publishing Directorate's website at https://armypubs.army.mil/ or see the company publications clerk.

CALL publications. Download and print or order hard copies from the CALL website at https://call2.army.mil/Login.aspx (authorized users only, CAC login required).

Recommended Publications

ATP 3-21.8, *Infantry Platoon and Squad,* 12 APR 2016. This ATP discusses basic troop-leading procedures (TLPs) and patrolling information.

FM 7-0, *Train to Win in a Complex World*, 05 OCT 2016. This FM details training management.

CALL 7-08, *Home Station Training Handbook,* 29 MAR 2017. This handbook outlines lessons learned and best practices for home-station training.

TC 3-22.9, *Rifle and Carbine,* 13 MAY 2016. This TC discusses training and qualification for the M4.

TC 3-22.249, *Light Machine Gun M249 Series,* 16 MAY 2017. This TC discusses training and qualification for the M249.

SUBMIT INFORMATION OR REQUEST PUBLICATIONS

To help you access information efficiently, the Center for Army Lessons Learned (CALL) posts publications and other useful products available for download on the CALL website:

http://call.army.mil

PROVIDE LESSONS AND BEST PRACTICES OR SUBMIT AN AFTER ACTION REVIEW (AAR)

If your unit has identified lessons or best practices or would like to submit an AAR or a request for information (RFI), please contact CALL using the following information:

Telephone: DSN 552-9569/9533; Commercial 913-684-9569/9533

Fax: DSN 552-4387; Commercial 913-684-4387

Mailing Address: **Center for Army Lessons Learned**
ATTN: Chief, Analysis Division
10 Meade Ave., Bldg. 50
Fort Leavenworth, KS 66027-1350

REQUEST COPIES OF CALL PUBLICATIONS

If you would like copies of this publication, please submit your request on the CALL restricted website (CAC login required):

https://call2.army.mil

Click on "Request for Publications." Please fill in all the information, including your unit name and street address. Please include building number and street for military posts.

NOTE: Some CALL publications are no longer available in print. Digital publications are available by clicking on "Publications by Type" under the "Resources" tab on the CALL restricted website, where you can access and download information. CALL also offers Web-based access to the CALL archives.

CALL produces the following publications on a variety of subjects:

- **Handbooks**
- **Bulletins, Newsletters, and Observation Reports**
- **Special Studies**
- ***News From the Front***
- **Training Lessons and Best Practices**
- **Initial Impressions Reports**

FOLLOW CALL ON SOCIAL MEDIA

https://twitter.com/USArmy_CALL
https://www.facebook.com/CenterforArmyLessonsLearned

COMBINED ARMS CENTER (CAC)
Additional Publications and Resources

The CAC home page address is: **http://usacac.army.mil**

Center for Army Leadership (CAL)

CAL plans and programs leadership instruction, doctrine, and research. CAL integrates and synchronizes the Professional Military Education Systems and Civilian Education System. Find CAL products at http://usacac.army.mil/cac2/cal.

Combat Studies Institute (CSI)

CSI is a military history think tank that produces timely and relevant military history and contemporary operational history. Find CSI products at http://usacac.army.mil/cac2/csi/csipubs.asp.

Combined Arms Doctrine Directorate (CADD)

CADD develops, writes, and updates Army doctrine at the corps and division level. Find the doctrinal publications at either the Army Publishing Directorate (APD) at http://www.apd.army.mil or the Central Army Registry (formerly known as the Reimer Digital Library) at http://www.adtdl.army.mil.

Foreign Military Studies Office (FMSO)

FMSO is a research and analysis center on Fort Leavenworth under the TRADOC G-2. FMSO manages and conducts analytical programs focused on emerging and asymmetric threats, regional military and security developments, and other issues that define evolving operational environments around the world. Find FMSO products at http://fmso.leavenworth.army.mil.

Military Review (MR)

MR is a revered journal that provides a forum for original thought and debate on the art and science of land warfare and other issues of current interest to the U.S. Army and the Department of Defense. Find MR at http://usacac.army.mil/cac2/militaryreview.

TRADOC Intelligence Support Activity (TRISA)

TRISA is a field agency of the TRADOC G-2 and a tenant organization on Fort Leavenworth. TRISA is responsible for the development of intelligence products to support the policy-making, training, combat development, models, and simulations arenas.

Capability Development Integration Directorate (CDID)

CDID conducts analysis, experimentation, and integration to identify future requirements and manage current capabilities that enable the Army, as part of the Joint Force, to exercise Mission Command and to operationalize the Human Dimension. Find CDID at http://usacac.army.mil/organizations/mccoe/cdid.

Joint Center for International Security Force Assistance (JCISFA)

JCISFA's mission is to capture and analyze security force assistance (SFA) lessons from contemporary operations to advise combatant commands and military departments on appropriate doctrine; practices; and proven tactics, techniques, and procedures (TTP) to prepare for and conduct SFA missions efficiently. JCISFA was created to institutionalize SFA across DOD and serve as the DOD SFA Center of Excellence. Find JCISFA at https://jcisfa.jcs.mil/Public/Index.aspx.

Support CAC in the exchange of information by telling us about your successes so they may be shared and become Army successes.

CPSIA information can be obtained
at www.ICGtesting.com
Printed in the USA
BVHW030455220821
614661BV00003BA/61

9 781678 184230